SHOWCASE OF INTERIOR DESIGN™

Midwest Edition II

Vitae Publishing, Inc.
Grand Rapids, MI

Published in the United States
by Vitae Publishing, Inc.
50 Monroe Avenue NW
Suite 400
Grand Rapids, MI 49503
(800)284-8232

Library of Congress
Cataloging-in-Publication Data

Showcase of Interior Design, Midwest Edition

p. cm.
Includes indexes.
ISBN 0-9624596-7-4
ISBN 1-883065-00-3 (soft)
1. Interior decoration-Midwest States-History-20th Century.
I. Elaine Markoutsas
NK2004.S53 1993 747.2171—dc20 93-21916 CIP

VITAE PUBLISHING, INC.

CHAIRMAN—JOHN C. AVES
PRESIDENT—JAMES C. MARKLE
DIRECTOR—GREGORY J. DEKKER

MIDWEST EDITION PRODUCTION STAFF

Communications Coordinators - Cynthia A. Vandecar
and Christine A. Humes
Publisher - Maria C. Cutler
Publisher - Ronald E. Frey
Publisher - Gita M. Gidwani
Publisher - Patty Stevens
Publisher - Paula Veseley
Contributing Author - Elaine Markoutsas

AVES, INCORPORATED

Production Artist—Nancy J. Allen
Production Supervisor—Douglas Koster
Inquiry Management—Jill Nabozny
Financial Management—Robert Spaman and Jeanne Seaman

Printed in Singapore by Toppan
Typeset in USA by Vitae Publishing, Inc.

Title page interior design: The Green Frog
Photo: J. Miles Wolf

Prologue

The book you are holding in your hands is proof positive that there are many fine and far sighted interior designers in the Midwestern United States. Many of these designers appeared in the very first printing of this book. This is the first revision of the Midwest Showcase of Interior Design. After the book first appeared in the Midwest, we proceeded to publish similar editions on the East Coast, the Pacific and then the South. We have come full circle, completing four regional editions which together cover the entire United States and now we have begun to publish updated revisions in each region.

The Second Edition of Midwest Showcase of Interior Design is twice as useful as the first book we printed in 1989. This book contains more than twice as many pages of inspiring interior images, more than twice the number of designers, a larger page format, and the book is being distributed around the world.

The reader will find scores of images that will ignite hundreds more fresh ideas. An idea about how you want to live is ephemeral and precious. We recommend that our readers enlist the members of our interior design braintrust to create their perfect habitat.

The concept for this publishing service started in Grand Rapids, Michigan, the nest of many ideas which have added luster to the design industry. The American Society of Interior Designers (ASID) was launched in Grand Rapids and the Foundation for Interior Designer Education and Research (FIDER) was also founded and is still headquartered here. We are therefore donating part of the proceeds from the domestic sale of this book to the Foundation for Interior Design Education and Research (FIDER), whose professional goals are supported by this publication. We are building bridges of information between designers and consumers which will enhance the selection process. ■

John C. Aves

TABLE OF CONTENTS

Just The Best Survives In The Heartland

By Elaine Markoutsas

From the rustic barns and silos that dot so much of its rural landscape to elegant turn-of-the-century urban brownstones and streamlined high-rises in its cities, Midwest architecture represents a curious amalgam of styles.

In Des Moines or Milwaukee, Indianapolis or Minneapolis, Chicago, Detroit or Cleveland, buildings with 19th century roots coexist with those expressing 20th century innovation. And within its homes thrives a melting pot of design, a synthesis of styles from the Old Countries, folk art that is purebred American, occasional whimsy and personality that speaks to the Heartland.

Visitors to the Midwest most often are struck by the friendliness of its people. How Midwesterners live—whether in graceful brick Queen Anne buildings, gingerbread Victorians with spacious front porches, lofts in converted factories, sprawling suburban ranches, country cottages or farmhouses—is an utter reflection of that warmth.

Although the avant-garde from the East and West Coasts might dismiss Midwest style as bland and flat as the land and its interior design as lacking guts, there's a lot to be said for it.

For one thing, it's secure.

"My clients are aware of the trends," said Chicago interior designer Dale Carol Anderson. "They choose not to follow them."

Or perhaps, they assimilate them.

"If a trend can make it over the Rockies in the West and over the Appalachians in the East," said Michael Walsh, president of Designer Previews, a designer referral service based in Chicago, "Midwesterners will consider it and adapt it as

OPPOSITE: Sublette Design Group — Translucent, full-height draperies allow light to filter through, softening two stories of dramatic windows.

their own. They're much less subject to fashionable decorating ideas. Most people in the Midwest decorate for the long term. It's not something they do every year. Consequently, they put a high priority on timelessness in terms of furniture."

To most, that translates as conservative.

"There's an essential conservatism that says, 'I don't want this unless I've seen it,'" said Janet Schirn, "'I don't want it unless my mother or my friends have it.'"

"Midwesterners are more traditional," said Jack Kreitinger. "They reject anything they think of as being trendy."

"People in the Midwest do tend to be more cautious," said Linda Coleman, president of Portfolio, a Chicago-based designer referral service. "They don't take the kinds of chances that people do on either coasts."

The conservative label has stuck like a thorn. Design in the Midwest often is underrated and overlooked, especially by slick, bicoastally-based shelter publications seeking the bold if not the beautiful. But not all agree that the term is pejorative.

"It doesn't mean that Midwesterners are boring," said Kreitinger. "But they have a sort of underlying practicality."

"It's not middle of the road design," said Larry Deutsch. "It can be very refined, infused with a sense of dignity and quality. There's a good balance of styles."

Which means that it's rare to find Midwest style going to extremes.

"There's not the flash of the West Coast," said Deutsch, "or the drama of the East Coast. Midwesterners are not trying to prove anything. They don't want to spend money for the sake of spending it."

"The Midwestern attitude is that our clients don't want people to think they've spent a lot of money," said Minneapolis designer Billy Beson. "They want style, good taste, but they don't want it to look like they tried too hard."

In other words, Midwesterners want their design to be classy, distinctive, and, yes, even drop-dead gorgeous. But, ssshhh, don't tell anybody.

"We design homes for our clients," said Deutsch, "not for their friends. A lot of people don't even want their homes photographed."

"Comfort is a very high priority," says Richard Himmel. "Knocking someone's socks off is farther down the list."

But don't call us Midwesterners provincial, either.

"We don't sell many parrot-and-palm tree prints in Minneapolis," said Beson, "but that doesn't mean you'll see ducks and pine trees instead. People here are sophisticated."

Indeed. Midwesterners are every bit as traveled as their West and East Coast cousins, and while they may not have the breadth of resources that both coasts boast, there are fine museums, art and antique galleries, design centers and even a formidable auction house, Leslie Hindman, in Chicago which set records in 1992 with the likes of a van Gogh discovered in Milwaukee that got snapped up for $1.43 million.

Richard Himmel once defined Midwest style not in terms of decorating but in its honest attitude, its "solidity and straightforwardness." Said Himmel: "It's a more tailored look."

But to a Midwesterner, tailored doesn't mean buttoned up or stuffy.

"Midwesterners are very relaxed in their approach to designing their homes," said Arlene Semel. "They don't want to lose the sense of themselves. They want an environment that speaks to family values, to comfortable living, to putting one's feet up.

"There are plenty of choices and room for individuality that says we don't have to copy," said Arlene Semel. "It's part of a pioneer spirit that relates to being a Midwesterner."

"How To Select And Manage Your Dream Weaver"

Home conjures a rich tapestry of images, an embodiment of our dreams. But most of us need help pulling the threads together, weaving into empty spaces an almost indefinable essence that is inviting.

Good interior designers and architects are dream weavers. They gather our fantasies, along with the collections and objects we hold dear, then they shape them, mixing them into a setting that's as cozy as sinking into a down-plumped sofa. We may not know a bergère from a torchère, but that's okay. Design professionals are masters of the vocabulary and how to use it. They know how to draw out a style that reflects what we're about and show us the kinds of furnishings that best fit it.

Why do we need designers to do that?

For one thing, few of us are confident enough to dress naked rooms, to cherrypick sofas and chairs, tables and lamps, fabrics and accessories, with the assurance that scale, style, pattern and color will work in the architecture of a space. And few of us are really adept at positioning all of the elements so that they make perfect design sense, both visually and functionally.

And then there are the details, the finishing touches from frescoed walls to lush chenille throws to specifications you may never have thought about. How thick should the glass top of a cocktail table be? What kind of edge? Pencil? Ogee? With a bevel or without? What size lamp shade? What shape? What material? To fringe or not fringe a pillow? What color threads? How thick? How long? Should the sofa be piped or welted for accent? In the same or contrasting fabric? Should the marble fireplace surround be honed or polished? These kinds of details clearly are time-consuming, yet they often are what set an interior apart.

OPPOSITE: Terrell Goeke Associates Inc. — Careful juxtaposition of natural and artificial lighting helps draw the eye to multiple layers of shapes and textures in this great room.

While we usually have a sense of what we like and don't like, honing in on our tastes is easier with a design professional who may corroborate our stylistic instincts or introduce us to an idiom that we may never have considered.

Designers also share with us their technical knowledge.

"Part of what we give clients," says Larry Deutsch, "is our knowledge of the history of the past in terms of styles and periods, as well as the ability to interpret with a sense of balance, a sense of proportion and eclecticism."

"Most clients come to designers for some level of educational experience," said Janet Schirn. "Designers have a greater knowledge of what goes into a successful living or working environment and a far greater knowledge of the possibilities. I recently sent a client six alternative floor plans, and she was stunned at the possibilities for furniture arrangement alone."

Besides orchestrating livable layouts, design professionals can put together sensible (and safe) lighting plans and advise on what fabrics will hold up for upholstery or whether certain stones are too porous to be laid in a high-traffic entry. They share their field expertise, their vast resources, their eye for ferreting out the right stuff, and equally important, their troubleshooting skills.

Even if we had the time and know-how to hunt down the furniture, lighting, fabric, flooring, carpeting, paint and wallcoverings that transform mere buildings into homes and office spaces into tasteful, welcoming workplaces, could we really handle the task of supervising the electrician, tile setter, upholsterer, painter, and paperhanger? Would we really want to?

"Designers take the risk out of decorating," says Michael Walsh, co-owner of Decorator Previews, a designer-referral service in Chicago. "They make sure the vanity fits, and that the sofa will come in the front door."

Dollar for dollar, designers ultimately can

save their clients a lot of money.

"The truth is," says Larry Deutsch, "men and women do not need more than a bed in which to sleep and a surface on which to put a few possessions. Everything after that becomes *want* not *need*. Clever design, like a fabulous movie set, can be done on a shoestring. But lasting design is expensive. That's why you need a designer."

There's a lot of substance besides style to interior design. And there may be a multitude of headaches, too. But if a table is delivered in the wrong size and finish, the designer assumes the liability, assuring that it will be shipped

BELOW: Anna Meyers Interiors Ltd.—An airy sitting cove adjacent to the grand entry of a European-style residence provides an inviting spot for listening to the birds that frequent an adjoining courtyard.

back to the manufacturer and returned to the client according to proper specifications. If you were on your own, you'd live with it or foot the freight bill - and take up a phone or fax battle to get it done right. If a measurement error was yours, you'd be plain out of luck.

Beyond what is available through conventional resources - design centers, retail stores, art galleries, antique shops and specialty boutiques - designers also have access to their own work rooms, craftsmen and artisans who can customize everything from bookcases to lamps.

While these are some of the compelling reasons for hiring a designer, some people still find the notion disconcerting.

Designer John Saladino once told *HG:* "People are petrified of me, scared I'll say something cruel and be judgmental . . . I tell them that I don't bite the first two or three times."

People do have many fears. They fret that they don't have enough money to spend or that their project will exceed their budget. They're afraid about losing their identity to a designer who may imprint their home with swags, jabots and jazzy objets d'art that say more about the designer than the client.

But not to worry. Among the more than 200,000 designers in the United States, you're bound to find the right one for you. It just might take a little time.

Today, more than ever, it's a matter of comparison shopping. Just as we search for quality, the best look and the best buy in shopping for an automobile or home, we're not likely to hire the first designer to trot out a portfolio.

Besides, responding to examples of a designer's work, whether it's 18th century English country or 20th century Miesian minimalism, personalities must click. You're not going to hand over thousands of dollars to someone you don't trust. And you'll want to be very forthright about how much money you intend to spend.

The designer-client relationship is a fairly

Carol R. Knott Interior Design — Generously proportioned French doors invite the outdoors to share in the casual comfort of a cozy sun room.

intimate one. The designer, after all, unravels the secrets within a home. What's in the medicine cabinet, the pantry, the closets? How well behaved are the kids? Are you fastidious to a fault or a shameless slouch when it comes to tidying up? What side of the bed does your mate claim? Does the dog curl up on the couch?

Where To Begin Looking.

Choosing the right designer, one sensitive to your needs, can be as daunting as finding the perfect soulmate. There are several ways to go.

Local or national publications may be wonderful leads, as they feature a slice of a designer's work for a particular client with a particular point of view. Designer showhouses allow a real walk-through of different styles that reflect sheer fantasy or a lifelike interpretation of a mythical client's ideals.

Word of mouth is another option. Endorsements from friends may be valid, but remember that even if you like the way your friend's home turned out, that doesn't mean you'll get along swimmingly with the designer.

Professional organizations such as the American Society of Interior Designers and the International Society of Interior Designers may be happy to provide you with the names of their members to interview. Bear in mind that fairness often requires them to rotate recommendations from membership lists. Also, most can't take the time to really connect styles and personalities. So odds of teaming up with one of their three recommendations may be slim.

Designer referral services take more of a matchmaking approach. For example, Designer Previews and Portfolio, both in Chicago, represent rosters of prescreened, qualified and reputable designers and architects. For a fee of about $100 to $200, they set up a consultation during which they assess the client's style and budget requirements. Through slides and photographs, they get a sense of what may work and recommend three designers/architects for the job.

But it's the one-on-one meeting that usually speaks volumes. Before you make an appointment to interview a prospective designer or architect, a little homework is in order.

Crystalize Goals For Your Project.

Think about what you want to do in your home or office. This sounds easy, but many people don't reconcile the desired end result - the look - with the way things must work - the function. In short, they fail to prioritize, a critical step in any design project.

In a kitchen rehab, for example, how you

use the space should be considered before style. Think about how you cook and how much counter space you need. Consider your storage needs and how specialized you want them to be. Do you want tray and cutlery dividers? Would you like an organized allotment for spices? Do you need two cooktops? These are but a few of the questions you'll need to ask yourself.

Go through every room that you plan to redesign and think about the furniture and accessories you'd like to keep, replace, add to. Establish a realistic budget. What is your absolute cap on spending? Determine what you can't live without. Would you rather splurge on one fantastic antique and hold back on fabrics or other pieces? Would you prefer to layer in - that is, develop a master plan that allows purchasing over a period of time - what you love, not just what you find?

Then, go through shelter magazines and

BELOW: John Robert Wiltgen Design Inc. — An 18th century Italian bibliotheque serves as the focal point of a living room that draws on a mix of design, track, recessed and spot lighting to highlight an extensive collection of art and antiques.

Larry N. Deutsch Interiors LTD.— Louis XV bronze sconces and a George III period scarlet japanned tall case clock highlight a wood-paneled gallery from the 1930s.

clip your favorite rooms. A picture may be worth a thousand words, but show two people the same photo and one might exclaim, "Oh, those colors are bright!" while another scoffs, "They're not bright enough!" One might say, "Don't you like this French furniture?" and another might answer, "That's not French." Your description might be limited by your design knowledge and ability to verbalize what you see.

"Few people have the degree of visualization that designers have," says Janet Schirn. "Almost no one reads a plan three-dimensionally."

But designer Dale Carol Anderson doesn't feel that's necessarily a handicap. "You don't have to verbalize or even visualize. All you have to do is identify through photos what you want in your home. Find pictures of rooms that would make you feel happy and warm."

Study an image and try to dissect it. What is it that really appeals to you? Is it the overall mood? Is it the color palette? How would you describe the room? The style of furnishings? Can you identify a common thread? The more you know, the easier it will be for you to talk about what you want.

"I look for some homogeny (in client photos)," says Janet Schirn, "the same overall color, contrasts and scale."

Be frank. If you really hate yellow, speak up. Don't be talked into something that makes you cringe. Don't be swayed by trends.

Discuss your expectations and how you see yourself living five years from now. Designers will appreciate a prospective client's effort to communicate articulately and in an organized fashion, just as the client will the designer's.

When you're speaking with prospective designers, you should observe their personal style, which says a lot about who they are and how they work. Review their education and hands-on experience, as well as their professional credentials. Knowing that a designer has passed a rigorous exam to earn a professional affiliation may be reassuring on one level, but don't rule out someone who appears to have a natural flair as well as a demonstrated ability to execute designs.

How do the designers or architects you're considering present themselves? Do you feel intimidated? At ease? Is their approach businesslike? Are they really listening to you?

How Designers Charge For Their Services.

Listening is especially important when it comes to budget. Understanding a designer's or architect's fee structure is critical. And, be firm about how much you have to spend.

Design fees generally represent a combination of methods. An hourly charge can range from $75 to $250. The range usually reflects the amount of experience a designer has. Design firms generally employ a sliding scale, and staff members with lesser experience command a lower fee. Drafting, for example, might be billed at $35 to $65 an hour. The upper end usually is reserved for consultation only - say, for example, hiring a designer for the purchase of art and antiques.

The hourly fee may be combined with a charge for products, usually 30 percent or 40 percent above the designer's cost. Sometimes designers charge straight retail - or work down from retail. If a sofa retails for $5,000, for example, it

Winnie Levin Interiors Ltd. — Deep raspberry walls and distinctive period furnishings create an opulent mood in the master bedroom suite of a Georgian estate.

might be billed at 30 percent off, or $3,500 (plus local taxes). Some designers also charge a flat fee or retainer for the project, which may represent a percentage of the estimated job costs.

Ultimately, the designer with whom you choose to work must be simpatico with you and your budget.

When you review the designer's portfolio, do you feel at ease with what you've seen? Even if the style you dream of isn't represented, do you feel the designer can translate your ideas? If you're not making major architectural changes, will the recommended design style suit the surroundings?

While it's not always possible to see a designer's work firsthand (it is, after all, an imposition on clients), it's acceptable to ask for references. Speak to them about their experience with a design or architectural firm. You might ask: Were you satisfied with the project? What was the best thing about working with the designer? Did the designer adhere to your budget? How long did it take to get the project done? Did you feel that was a reasonable amount of time? Was the job done to your expectations? Does it really reflect you?

Once you've made a decision, formalize it with a written contract. The collaborative design process then begins, usually with interior plans, architectural blueprints and a series of shopping expeditions. That's the fun part.

Being a part of the design process is extremely rewarding. As you work with your designer, you collaborate on decisions that will enhance your lifestyle. The result will be a home that will make you proud.

This book, *Showcase of Interior Design,* can be a treasure trove. Besides offering a voyeuristic glimpse into a variety of environments that represent diverse talents and styles, it provides a wealth of useful information about the professionals featured, including their philosophy; their residential and commercial clients; their education, awards and professional affiliations; and the publications in which they've appeared.

Studying various styles and approaches will guide you in understanding what best complements you.

The *Showcase of Interior Design* can be your first step in making a very important choice. Clicking with the right designer will send you on a special odyssey through fields of dreams. And ultimately, it will lead you home.

BY ELAINE MARKOUTSAS

Elaine Markoutsas writes a syndicated design column that appears in nearly 250 newspapers nationwide. She is also a field editor for Meredith Corp., whose stable of publications includes *Better Homes & Gardens*, *Country Home* and *Traditional Home*. Elaine's previous experience includes positions as design editor for *The Chicago Tribune Sunday Magazine* and director of home furnishings for The Merchandise Mart. A graduate of Northwestern University, she lives in Chicago with her husband, Charles Leroux, and son, Evan.

BELOW: Janet Schirn Design Group—Designed to serve one or two occupants equally as well as large groups, this living room achieves an aura of refinement without appearing stuffy.

Akins and Aylesworth, Ltd.

MARILYN AKINS, ASID
DONNA AYLESWORTH, ISID
30 EAST FIRST STREET
HINSDALE, IL 60521
(708)325-3355

We love clear color, sometimes using it boldly, sometimes softly, always considering what colors are most flattering to the client. We aim for warmth and comfort, preferring to accessorize with antiques. Although creativity is our forté we pride ourselves in being good business people as well. ■

CREDENTIALS:
Marilyn Akins:
ASID

Donna Aylesworth:
ISID

■ *Our approach to design considers the client's personality and lifestyle, as well as the architecture, in determining the style direction of the project. We like to enhance the client's taste preferences and raise them to a level beyond which even the most sophisticated client may have imagined.*

ALAN PORTNOY INTERIORS LTD., ASID

ALAN PORTNOY
440 NORTH WELLS STREET
CHICAGO, IL 60610
(312)828-0266

PROJECTS:
Private Residences: Chicago and surrounding suburbs; La Costa, California; and Del Ray, Boca Raton, North Miami, Miami and Ft. Lauderdale, Florida.

CREDENTIALS:
ASID, Member
Art Institute of Chicago, BFA

PUBLISHED IN:
Chicago Sun Times
Chicago Tribune
Windows Beautiful
Northshore Magazine

■ *It is our philosophy that every home should possess a timeless beauty which reflects the lifestyle, personality, and taste of its owner. We measure our success of the past 25 years by the satisfied clientele for whom we have executed projects ranging from traditional, contemporary, hi-tech, to the blended styles of the eclectic. We take pride in our ability to incorporate optimum utilization of space, custom built-ins, architectural details, and lighting to create a canvas which satisfies the ambiance and comfort of our clients.* ■

THE ENGLISH WORLD
ANATOMY OF A CLOUD

Dale Carol Anderson Ltd.

DALE ANDERSON, ASID
2030 NORTH MAGNOLIA AVENUE
CHICAGO, IL 60614
(312)348-5200 FAX (312)348-5271

I am equally comfortable producing sleek contemporary, as well as Old World traditional interiors. Good design is synthesis — combining the needs of the client, the architecture and site, the craftsmen and artisans — all to execute the concepts developed by the client and myself. My projects are client and site specific, each is therefore unique. The only constant from project to project is that of timelessness and quality in concept, materials and workmanship. I believe attention to detail separates a quality design project from all others, and my clients clearly require this. ■

Anna Meyers Interiors Ltd.

ANNA MEYERS
162 WEST HURON
CHICAGO, IL 60610
(312)751-1010 FAX (312)751-9002

■ *Whether one room or an entire house, we visualize the whole — how it all works together — and offer a plan to make it happen. We understand every present has a past. Together, we carefully edit what you can live with, work with, and what you want to keep.*

Good design is about detail. It's about comfort. It's about beautiful surroundings. What begins with an interview ends with the installation, but the respect and mutual benefits last a lifetime. ■

PROJECTS:
Private Residences: Manhattan and Long Island, New York; Athens, Greece; Palm Springs, California; Traverse City and New Buffalo, Michigan; and Chicago, Illinois.

Commercial Work: Corporate offices and industrial plants. Leaps & Bounds, Inc.; Price Waterhouse; Cozzi Iron & Metal, Inc.; Brandenburg Industrial Service Company; and Sun Chemical Corp.

CREDENTIALS:
Harrington Institute of Interior Design
DePaul University
Park Ridge Youth Campus Showcase, 1987, 1988, 1989
Woman's American ORT Showcase House, 1992, 1993
House Beautiful Seminar Panel Member, 1993
Celebrating over 17 years of successful work in the interior design industry

PUBLISHED IN:
The Chicago Tribune
Chicago Magazine
Chicago Sun Times
Window Coverings Magazine
Log Home Living
Various other national publications

BELOW: Converted four story apartment building to single family residence. Antique stained glass panels used to keep space open and yet define dining room.

LEFT: Original space ended at column, extended ten feet to gain first floor sitting area with green house above.

BELOW: Fireplace detail: Sandblasted glass by Mark Milenowsky. Artwork by Zhou Ling.

ARCH ASSOCIATES/STEPHEN GUERRANT, AIA

MARCIA GUERRANT, ASID
824 PROSPECT AVENUE
WINNETKA, IL 60093
(708) 446-7810 FAX (708) 446-7818

My personal objective is to interpret my client's taste and needs in the most creative and resourceful way. I hope that each project completed is unique from others and is a true reflection of my client's desired lifestyle.

As much as interior design is a creative process, it is also a service business. While making the design process an exciting and enjoyable experience for my clients, my commitment to effective communication and attention to detail ensures final success and satisfaction. ■

PROJECTS:
Private Residences: Chicago and North Shore areas of Illinois; Palm Springs, California; Marco Island, Boca Raton and Stuart, Florida; Lake areas of Wisconsin and Michigan; New York, New York; Philadelphia, Pennsylvania and Deer Valley, Utah.

CREDENTIALS:
ASID, Professional Member
Elmira College, Elmira, New York
In practice as the Interior Design Group of Arch Associates since 1980

PUBLISHED IN:
Better Homes and Gardens
Remodeling Ideas
Kitchen and Bath Ideas
Decorating Ideas
Southern Living, Creative Ideas for Living
Woman's World
The Chicago Tribune

ABOVE: Family room adjacent to parlor of elegant Victorian home.

LEFT: Snug and tiny country-style guest bedroom.

OPPOSITE: Vacation condominium in Deer Valley, Utah, with rustic Western ambience.

Arlene Semel & Associates, Inc.

ARLENE SEMEL, ASID
445 NORTH FRANKLIN STREET
CHICAGO, IL 60610
(312)644-1480 FAX (312)644-8157

We take the client's dream and with imagination and experience create a reality well beyond their hopes and expectations.

PROJECTS:
Private Residences: Chicago's Gold Coast and North Shore, Illinois; New York; Los Angeles, California; Detroit, Michigan; Racine, Wisconsin and Westport, Connecticut.

Vacation and secondary residences: Cable, Wisconsin; New Buffalo, Michigan; Aspen, Colorado; Nantucket, Massachusetts and Boca Raton, Florida.

Commercial Work: Professional offices, health clubs, model apartments, private yachts and consulting to residential real estate developers.

PUBLISHED IN:
House Beautiful
Better Homes and Gardens
Bedroom & Bath Ideas
Decorating Remodeling Magazine
Interior Design
Chicago Magazine
Chicago Tribune
Chicago Sun Times
Crain's Chicago Business
North Shore Magazine

GILMORE-ASHFORD-POWERS DESIGN, INC.

CALVIN ASHFORD JR., ISID, OBD
505 NORTH LAKE SHORE DRIVE
SUITE 210
CHICAGO, IL 60611
(312)644-9567 FAX (312)644-9566

■ *Our firm's focus is to design environments that adapt to people, rather than people adapting to the design.* ■

PROJECTS:
Private Residences: Chicago, New York, Palm Springs and many other cities throughout the United States, Great Britain and Canada.

Commercial Work: Yachts, aircraft, AT&T Credit Union, LPT Partnership, Laracris Co. and the award winning offices of J.B. Industrials in London.

CREDENTIALS:
Columbia University
University of Michigan
Residential Design Excellence Award, Chicago Design Source and Merchandise Mart, 1990
Designer of the Year, BIDA
Steward Award for Creative Design, 1988
Who's Who in Interior Design, 1990

PUBLISHED IN:
Interior Design
HG
Metropolitan Home
Better Homes and Gardens
Ebony
Chicago Sun Times
Chicago Tribune
New York Times
Great Bathrooms by Jeffery Weiss

Design team for projects were:
Norbert Young, Project Manager
Duane Boxx, Project Manager
Melanie Amos, Designer
Keith Moore, Designer

BELOW: The black granite floor and clear glass cocktail table are focus points of this celebrity client's contemporary town apartment.

OPPOSITE: This custom designed lucite and brass staircase makes a dramatic statement in the same client's second home — an 8,000 square foot country estate.

B.R. Design, Inc.

BUSHRA RAHIM, ASID
28001 CHAGRIN BOULEVARD, SUITE 103
CLEVELAND, OH 44122
(216)831-1510 FAX(216)831-1615

Homes reflect people—their personalities and life styles. That is what I try to capture in my work. Through a close relationship with my clients, I interpret their needs and desires into an integral part of the design. By combining exquisite fabric, colors and attention to detail, I aim to create ambiance of timeless quality and international elegance.

Working with architecture of old and new homes is my most exciting challenge. To transform spaces into an imaginative classic or contemporary atmosphere of beauty, function and creativity is my forte. ■

PROJECTS:
Private Residences: Toronto, Canada; McLean, Virginia; Clinton, Iowa and Cleveland, Ohio.

Commercial Work: Southwest General Hospital; St. Alexis Hospital; Elyria Memorial Hospital and many physician offices in Cleveland, Ohio.

CREDENTIALS:
ASID, Member
Baghdad University, Iraq, BA
Cuyahoga Community College, Associates Degree in Interior Design
Cancer Society Hope House Showcase, 1989,1992

SHEILA BARRON INTERIORS

SHEILA BARRON
602 MICHIGAN
EVANSTON, IL 60202
(708)864-4778

BELOW: Traditional Home "1992 Design Award" reprinted with permission of *Traditonal Home*© Magazine.

William Beson Interior Design

WILLAIM BESON, ASID
WILLIAM BESON INTERIOR DESIGN
INTERNATIONAL MARKET SQUARE
275 MARKET SQUARE, SUITE 540
MINNEAPOLIS, MN 55405
(612)338-8187 FAX (612)338-2462

RENEE LEJEUNE HALLBERG, ASID

■ *Our designers interpret the client's needs both practically and aesthetically to create the ideal environment. We pride ourselves in the versatility of our styles which enables us to work with clients from a contemporary "less is more" attitude to the lavish traditional interiors shown here. Our impeccable style is coupled with top notch service and a sense of integrity which constantly drives us to strive for the very best.* ■

BELOW: Faux marble walls create an excellent background for opulent detail. The warm color palette contributes to the welcoming ambiance.

PROJECTS:
Private Residences: Minneapolis and St. Paul, Minnesota; Aspen and Denver, Colorado; Palm Desert, California; Naples, Port Royal, Florida and Washington, D.C.

Commercial Work: Executive offices, law firms and hospitality.

CREDENTIALS:
William Beson:
ASID, Allied Member
"Star on the Horizon" award, Chicago Design Sources

Renee LeJeune Hallberg:
ASID, Allied Member

PUBLISHED IN:
Numerous national and local publications

LEFT: The evident attention to detail reflects the integrity of our design excellence.

BELOW: A blending of periods and styles support the use of varied patterns to create a feeling of sophisticated elegance.

L. B. Black Interior Design

LOIS BLACK
1134 WEST FARWELL
CHICAGO, IL 60626
(312)761-9029

■ *I see interior design as a partnership: My client provides me a history of life experience, memories and feelings; I offer my client an appreciation of the architectural space, a sense of scale and a knowledge of resources which serve to expand the client's horizons. Together we create a vision of what is possible and work together to produce an environment in which the client feels truly at home.* ■

Lawrence Boeder Interior Design

LAWRENCE BOEDER
445 EAST WISCONSIN
LAKE FOREST, IL 60045
(312)613-6640

Most of my work involves traditional, understated design. My staff and the range of talented craftsmen I employ as resources, appreciate the need for quality and beauty. The result we are seeking is comfortable and never dated. Happily, each project is as distinctive as each client's own personality and lifestyle. ■

ABOVE TOP: Traditional residential setting.

ABOVE: For homes in Lake Forest, Illinois.

OPPOSITE: Special setting where antiques, collectibles and pieces come together in a Lake Bluff, Illinois home.

Alexander V. Bogaerts & Associates/Architecture/Interior Design

ALEXANDER V. BOGAERTS, AIA
2445 FRANKLIN ROAD
BLOOMFIELD HILLS, MI 48302
(313)334-5000

Over 25 years ago, I recognized that each project is unique in terms of its space and client needs; and in order to continuously seek design excellence, the design concept must respond to those factors and not be preconceived or forced.

The unique character of floor area and shape, ceiling heights and slopes, natural light and scale greatly influence the design philosophy of a project. The cognition of these factors, and the focused resolve to continuously enhance and refine the determined design to an artful scale and proportion are absolutely essential. This unending attention to detail, and the willingness to create bold and innovative concepts provides my clients with designs which are contemporary, unique, comfortable and of lasting design character. ■

PROJECTS:
Private Residences: Bloomfield Hills, Birmingham, West Bloomfield and Troy Michigan.

Commercial Work: A substantial number of office, medical and retail projects.

CREDENTIALS:
AIA, Member
Bachelor of Architecture, Lawrence Technological University
Design Awards: City of Novi, Michigan; City of Southfield, Michigan.

PUBLISHED IN:
Detroit Monthly Magazine
The Detroit News
Oakland Press
Birmingham Eccentric
Detroit Free Press

Bridget Havey Interiors

BRIDGET HAVEY
7558 WOODLAND COURT
BURR RIDGE, IL 60525
(708) 246-9181

■ *A home should be a place where comfort, style and relaxation are first and foremost. Through interpretation, editing and creativity, these abstract ideas are combined to form aesthetically pleasing solutions. I enjoy avoiding the "happy medium" and delight in a daring and unconventional approach.* ■

PROJECTS:
Private Residences: Numerous projects in Illinois: Burr Ridge, Hinsdale, La Grange, Western Springs, Darien, Claredon Hills, Glen Ellyn, Orland Park and Palos Park; Michigan and Indiana.

Commercial Work: Various professional offices, hospitals, model homes and retail store display.

CREDENTIALS:
Hinsdale Decorators Showcase House, 1989-1992
Studio Bagatelle
Park Ridge Youth Campus Showcase House, 1993

PUBLISHED IN:
Chicago Tribune

Busch and Associates

F. MARIE BUSCH, ASID
1615 NORTH MOHAWK
CHICAGO, IL 60614
(312) 649-9106 FAX (312) 649-9106

My approach to interior design is to be individualistic, understanding, flexible and creative in meeting client needs. Much thought goes into the coloration of each assignment, as well as fabric selection, and where possible, architectural detailing, to establish comfortable and timeless grace for every client without repetition of design ideas. ■

PROJECTS:
Private Residences: Chicago and suburbs of Illinois; Telluride, Colorado; Long Boat Key and Naples, Florida; Scottsdale, Arizona; Atlanta, Georgia; California; Wisconsin; Michigan; Arkansas and London, England.

Commercial Work: First National Bank of Chicago, President McMaster-Carr, Phoschem, Valley Lo Sports Club, dental, attorney and corporate offices.

CREDENTIALS:
ASID, Vice President, Illinois Chapter, 1992-1993
ASID, Board Member, 1989-Current
Chicago Design Sources, Designer of the Year 1988
Bachelor of Fine Arts, Stephens College
Harrington Institute of Interior Design

PUBLISHED IN:
House and Garden
House Beautiful (one of the ten best showhouse rooms, 1989)
Chicago Tribune
Chicago Sun Times

OPPOSITE BELOW: "Cochise" the howling coyote sets the tone for this whimsy filled porch, a favorite summertime retreat.

OPPOSITE ABOVE: Capitalizing on an already dark room, the deep green walls create a serene setting for a smallish living room and present the perfect backdrop for "Hairdresser" a 1948 painting by Russian-born Simka Simkhovitch.

ABOVE: A large, sunny living room, made intimate by the use of dark green walls and dramatic shapes.

CLB Designs, Inc.

CARYN L. BURSTEIN
P.O. BOX 410335
ST. LOUIS, MO 63141
(314)991-3232 FAX(314)991-3565

CLB Designs, Inc. was formed to create an interior architectural design firm that intertwines the understanding and complexity of interior architecture and the simplistic yet creative elements of interior design. Both aspects of design coordinate together in order to form a unison which results with a complete and successful project. ■

PROJECTS:
Private Residences: Interior architecture and interior design for residences throughout the metropolitan St. Louis and St.Charles, Missouri areas.

Commercial Work: Various medical and dental offices; healthcare facilities; corporate and executive offices; clubhouses; banks; libraries; community college; retail and store designs in Chicago, O'Fallon and Godfrey, Illinois; Warwick, Rhode Island; LaJolla, California and Fort Smith, Arkansas.

CREDENTIALS:
University of Missouri - Columbia, BS emphasizing in Housing and Interior Design
Harvard University-Architectural Delineation Graduate School of Design

PUBLISHED IN:
St. Louis Homes and Gardens
Other local publications

BELOW OPPOSITE: A portion of the totally unfinished level now features this living space with all custom designed furnishings, entertainment unit, and decorative glass block wall creating a unique statement, while providing all the modern amenities for ultimate comfort in casual living and entertaining.

ABOVE OPPOSITE: The completely custom renovated kitchen enlarged to access the great room and redesigned for functional organized space utilizes gloss white laminate cabinetry with chrome accents and mirrored backsplashes to achieve a dramatic effect.

ABOVE: This overwhelming massive size room is now separated into four inviting individual custom designed conversation areas for reading, entertaining and lounging. The twelve foot custom designed see through fish tank allows for privacy between three areas while maintaining the room's visual impact.

Nancy Clough Interiors

NANCY CLOUGH, ISID
49 NORFOLK AVENUE
CLARENDON HILLS, IL 60514
(708)654-2478 FAX (708)654-2495

Rooms are meant to be living testimony of the individuality, personality and lifestyle of the client. Interpreting the needs of the client is the best way to ensure comfortable, completely unique projects. My keen attention to detail and commitment to being service oriented makes the project pleasurable.

I design rooms that have an aura of years of collecting and gathering. When the project is complete, it appears as if we have spent years accumulating each piece in the room. Combining the new with antiques, along with the client's favorite pieces, creates a room meant to be lived in.

Quality, integrity and creativity mark the spaces I have touched. ■

PROJECTS:
Private Residences and Commercial Work: Chicago and surrounding suburbs; Galena, Illinois; Grand Beach and Mackinac Island, Michigan; Buffalo, New York and Washington, D.C.

CREDENTIALS:
ISID, Professional Member
ISID Illinois Chapter, Board Member
Registered Interior Designer, State of Illinois
Michigan State University, BS in Interior Design, Magna Cum Laude
General Electric Lighting Institute
The International Academy of Merchandising and Design, Instructor
Designer Showhouses Hinsdale, Illinois
Design experience since 1964

PUBLISHED IN:
Better Homes and Gardens
Woman's Day
Victorian Sampler

ABOVE TOP: Wonderful natural materials and architectural repetition in the conservatory create a tranquil year-round haven for the family. The design for this room is specifically tailored to blend with the natural beauty outside. A combination of linen, iron, stone, glass and wood in neutral hues ties all of nature's elements together and draws the environment inside.

ABOVE BOTTOM: This guest room was designed to greet a friend or relative with a restful oasis. A pale background accented with vivid colors gives the overall ambiance evocative of a country garden at the height of midsummer.

OPPOSITE: Rich colors play against sumptuous formal vanilla draperies to create this comfortable, yet elegant English living room. Antique lamps, a hand painted table, needlepoint pieces and the owner's collection of antique brass candlesticks showcase quintessential English manor living.

Cricket Interiors

HELEN M. DEGULIS
2505 ARLINGTON ROAD
CLEVELAND HEIGHTS, OH 44118
(216)321-1565

■ *The project should be fun and the result should include as much of the client's personality, taste and artifacts as possible. As a life long student of art the skillful use of color is essential to my work. The finished design should be simple, classic, of the highest quality and respectful of the architecture, whether traditional or contemporary.* ■

PROJECTS:
Private Residences: Cleveland, Ohio area, Cleveland Heights, Shaker Heights, Pepper Pike, Waite Hill, Gates Mills and Daisy Hill; Tallahassee, Florida; New York; New Canaan, Connecticut, Short Hills, New Jersey and Chapel Hill, North Carolina.

Commercial Work: Private clubs, colleges and universities, law firms; in Cleveland, Ohio and New York City.

CREDENTIALS:
Notre Dame College of Ohio
Cleveland Museum of Art May Show
March of Dimes "Living in Space" Creativity Award
Decorator Showhouses, Cleveland area

D.D.I.

DARLENE DUDECK, ASID
1415 MEADOW LANE
GLENVIEW, IL 60025
(708) 998-1060 FAX (708) 998-1061

Function, aesthetics and attention to detail are all necessary elements of good design. A background in both contract and residential design has inspired me to place function at the foundation of every project. Quality materials and furnishings are

then superimposed on this foundation. These elements are integrated through an exchange of ideas with my client. The result is a design which reflects the needs, budget and personality of the client. Our interiors carry two signatures. ■

PROJECTS:
Private Residences: Chicago's Gold Coast, North Shore, Galena and other select areas of Illinois.

Commercial Work: Law offices, doctor's offices and country clubs.

Specialize In: Commodity trading firms.

CREDENTIALS:
ASID
IBD
AIA
First Place, "Best Design for the Electronic Office"

PUBLISHED IN:
Interiors
Managed Office Technology, 1986
Area Development, cover

Jackie Davis Interiors, Inc.

JACKIE DAVIS
3755 EAST 82ND STREET, SUITE 100
INDIANAPOLIS, IN 46240
(317) 577-1116 FAX (317) 578-1907

Jackie Davis Interiors, Inc. takes pride in having no "signature" style, but is known for its use of color and the solving of unique space planning problems.

Our designers seek to achieve the highest level of aesthetics and functionality, while working within each client's guidelines and project's limitations.

We share the belief that attention to detail, a striving for creative excellence and special follow-up service are the keys to each successful interior. ■

PROJECTS:
Private Residences and Vacation Homes: Indiana; Chicago, Illinois; New York; Florida and Michigan.

Commercial Work: Indianapolis Motor Speedway VIP suites; CEO's office of Logo 7; country clubs; sororities; banks and medical; legal and professional offices.

CREDENTIALS:
Staff of ASID affiliated designers
Gold Key & Designer's Choice Awards
St. Margaret's Guild Decorator's Showhouse

PUBLISHED IN:
Indianapolis Monthly

ABOVE OPPOSITE: A hand-painted trunk and memorabilia from many travels fill this den.

BELOW OPPOSITE: This living room's furnishings were placed to facilitate entertaining, conversation and recitals.

ABOVE: Dramatic architecture and accents of rose, yellow, periwinkle and black enrich the living/dining areas of this lakeside home.

The Design Dept., Inc.

DIANE KERN & CAROL LADER
21749 SHELBURNE ROAD
SHAKER HEIGHTS, OH 44122
(216)464-0622 FAX(216)591-0838

■ *Our work is guided by appropriateness to architecture and suitability to a client's lifestyle. By blending compatible elements in creative ways, we achieve a timeless design. Quality, good taste, experience and imagination dictate our solutions. Thoughtful communication and honesty between client and designer are vital to the design process.* ■

PROJECTS:
Private Residences: Ohio, Florida, New York and California.

Commercial Work: Corporate offices, law offices and medical suites.

CREDENTIALS:
Over thirty-five years of combined experience in interior design, lighting design, antiques and office interiors
W.R.U., School of Art and Architecture
C.W.R.U., Masters Studies Art History
Cleveland Institute of Art
Miami University
Conduct lectures in antiques and design

RICHARD MESNICK
3510 HAMPTON ROAD
PEPPER PIKE, OH 44122
(216)464-4778 FAX (216)360-0083

NATALIE GOTTFRIED

We allow our clients' personalities to dominate each project, giving our work a unique and ever-fresh appearance. Function is never sacrificed for style but beauty is never placed second to utility. In this way we create timeless interiors that provide a classic, comfortable environment for our diverse clientele. Our projects express a broad spectrum of both style and function as seen in our photographs of the plush legal office, spectacular high-tech bath/spa and cozy, yet dramatic great room. ■

PROJECTS:
Private Residences: Throughout Northeastern Ohio and South Florida.

Commercial Work:
Professional offices; clubs; shops; restaurants and hospitals throughout Northeastern Ohio.

CREDENTIALS:
ASID, Allied Practitioner
Carnegie Melon University
Cuyahoga Community College
Junior League Designer's Show House
American Cancer Society Designer Hope House

PUBLISHED IN:
Cleveland Press
Cleveland Plain Dealer
Sun Press
Chagrin Valley Times

Deutsch/Parker Design, Ltd.

LARRY N. DEUTSCH, ASID
WILLIAM F. PARKER, ASID
325 WEST HURON STREET, SUITE 500
CHICAGO, IL 60610
(312)649-1244 FAX (312)649-9617

The key to success is commitment to a set of principles based on achieving the highest level of professionalism. We work closely with in-house architects in order to design for the client's lifestyle and interpret those lifestyle needs selectively through fine art and furnishings. We believe that positive client communications, creative solutions and good business practices result in elegant design. ■

PROJECTS:
Private Residences: Chicago, Illinois' Gold Coast and North Shore; New York; Palm Beach and Jacksonville, Florida; Beverly Hills, Palm Springs and San Francisco, California; Scottsdale and Tucson, Arizona; Flat Head Lake, Montana and Casa de Campo, Dominican Republic.

Commercial Work: Retirement and geriatric centers, country clubs, hotels and restaurants, lobbies and executive offices.

CREDENTIALS:
Larry N. Deutsch, ASID:
National ASID Conference, Chairman, Chicago, 1984
Los Angeles, 1986
Outstanding Achievement in Design, The Merchandise Mart, Chicago, 1986
Dean of Design, The Merchandise Mart, Chicago, 1992

William F. Parker, ASID:
National Circle of Excellence Award, Ethan Allen, Inc.
ASID Arizona South Chapter, President, 1987,1988
ASID National Board of Directors, 1989-1990
First Place, ASID Arizona South Chapter Residential Design Award Competition, 1989, 1990

PUBLISHED IN:
Architectural Digest
HG
House Beautiful
Better Homes and Gardens
Chicago Tribune
North Shore Home & Design
Tucson Lifestyle
Arizona Republic
Arizona Daily Star

G. M. Doveikis & Associates, Inc.

GAIL MCINTOSH DOVEIKIS, ASID
2058 CONCOURSE DRIVE
ST. LOUIS, MO 63146
(314) 567-4944 FAX (314) 567-1270

Though many designers specialize in a particular style or look, I enjoy creating interiors that are as diverse as my clientele. Every client and home have unique characteristics that set them apart from others. Nothing pleases me more than to uncover each project's treasures and accentuate them in a way to truly capture the client's personal style.

To me, the secrets to successful design mirror those in any professional endeavor: ask relevant questions, listen carefully to the client, find creative solutions and provide excellent service with utmost attention to every detail. ■

PROJECTS:
Private Residences: Homes throughout the St. Louis, Missouri area, including Ladue, Town & Country, Creve Coeur, Clayton, Chesterfield and the Central West End.

Commercial Work: Numerous professional office suites, medical facilities and hospitals throughout the St. Louis, Missouri metropolitan area.

CREDENTIALS:
NCIDQ Certified
ASID, Professional Member since 1979
ASID, Missouri East Past Chapter Officer and Board Member
ASID, Missouri East Showhouse participant, 1986, 1990
ASID, Missouri East Presidential Citation, 1989
University of Missouri, Columbia, BS in Housing and Interior Design, Cum Laude

DuBay & Maire, Ltd.

ARCHITECTURE AND
INTERIOR DESIGN

DANIEL DuBAY
GREGORY MAIRE
445 NORTH WELLS STREET, SUITE 200
CHICAGO, IL 60610

Jayne Dranias Designs

JAYNE DRANIAS, ASID
1438 NORTH MONROE
RIVER FOREST, IL 60305
(708) 771-9352 FAX(312) 222-9091

■ *I strive for timelessness in design, working closely with clients and guiding them to achieve the best design for their lifestyle. Such as, introducing contemporary art and accessories into a traditional setting.*

After many years in the field of interior design, it has convinced me that quality and comfort are the most important features for timelessness! ■

PROJECTS:
Private Residences: Chicago, Oak Brook, River Forest, Winnetka and Lake Forest, Illinois; Boca Raton and Palm Beach Florida; New York City and Long Island, New York; Arizona; Lajolla, California; London, England and Athens, Greece.

Commercial Work: Corporate offices; insurance companies; law firms and restaurants.

CREDENTIALS:
ASID, Professional Member
Harrington School of Design
Northwestern University
The Crown Mansion Showcase House

PUBLISHED IN:
House Beautiful
House and Garden
Better Homes and Gardens
Ortho Educational Book
Architectural Digest Supplement
Many local and national periodicals

ABOVE TOP: Overlooking the vast vista of Lake Michigan, the unusual details of the oval sitting room with its quasi-Byzantine arches form a striking background for the contemporary furnishings and abstract art. The earthen tones of the monochromatic color scheme and minimal use of the varying textures create a strong unifying mood for this unusual setting.

ABOVE: This library combines regency, directoire and contemporary furniture for view of hearth over which hangs an antique portrait. The color scheme is keyed to the antique Persian area rug. Using cranberry striae wallcovering on the ceiling and book niches solidifies the light oak paneling. Please note that the herringbone parquet was placed on the diagonal as the area rug and furniture - highlighting the corner fireplace.

OPPOSITE: Elegant fabrics and richly toned walls complement the architecture of this magnificent room. English and French furniture combined with contemporary pieces create an aura of European grandeur. Fine antiques and art are reminiscent of the "grand tour."

Jane Frankel Interiors

JANE FRANKEL
27600 CHAGRIN BOULEVARD
CLEVELAND, OH 44122
(216) 464-6166 FAX (216) 464-6473

It is my belief that the basis for all great interior design begins with an understanding of a project's purpose and function.

Our work is highlighted by meticulous attention to detail incorporating quality furnishings and workmanship to create an atmosphere of intimacy, luxury and graciousness.

There is always an appreciation of order and architectural integrity, but in the end the rooms must shine with vitality and reflect the personality and image of the client. ■

PROJECTS:
Private Residences: Ohio; San Francisco, California; New York City, New York; Palm Beach, Florida; Washington, D.C.; Charlottesville, Virginia.

Commercial Work: The Country Club; Oakwood Club; Beechmont Country Club; corporate offices, boutiques and restaurants.

CREDENTIALS:
Hollins College, BA
Member of the Advisory Board to Interior Design Program at Kent State University
Interior Designer for nineteen years
Barron's Who's Who in Interior Design

PUBLISHED IN:
Showcase of Interior Design, Commercial Edition
Cleveland Magazine
The Plain Dealer
Northern Ohio Live

The Frey Company

RONALD E. FREY, ASID
RICHARD WHALLON
1514 WEALTHY STREET SE, SUITE 210
GRAND RAPIDS, MI 49506
(616)456-1220 FAX (616)456-7677

The Frey Company holds fast to the philosophy that the identity of their clients be projected in the interiors designed for them. They view the design process as an educational journey, integrating the client's needs with the appropriate elements of design. The ability to design in a broad range of styles, accompanied by a working relationship of integrity and trust, contributes to the successful completion of exciting and enduring interiors. ■

PROJECTS:
Private Residences: Michigan, Indiana, Illinois, Tennessee and Oregon.

Commercial Projects: Teknion Furniture Systems, World Headquarters Showroom, Toronto, Ontario; Nynex Business Centers, Nationwide; Betten Imports/Mercedes Benz, Grand Rapids, Michigan; Honda West, Holland, Michigan; and Mazda Great Lakes Training Facility, Kentwood, Michigan.

CREDENTIALS:
ASID, Professional Member
Major Room - Grand Rapids Symphony Showhouse/Brookby Estate
NCIDQ Certified
Kendall College of Art & Design, BFA, Interior Design, 1986
Adjunct Faculty Member, Kendall College of Art & Design
President, ASID Student Chapter, Kendall College of Art & Design, 1984
Feature Writer for *Cosmopolitan Home*
Who's Who in Interior Design

ABOVE: A backdrop of rich wood creates the perfect setting for combining diverse elements. Sisal flooring, leather wingback chairs and taffeta window treatments integrate for a relaxed traditional interior.

LEFT: Hand-painted walls, original watercolors, ceramic tile and tapestry fabric give this newly constructed bath an Old World charm.

OPPOSITE: Deep aubergine and regal gold complement the abundance of wood panels and help escort this room of heritage into the 90's.

PUBLISHED IN:
Cosmopolitan Home
New View
The Grand Rapids Press
Collectibles Market Guide
Trendway Furniture catalog and national advertisements
Asmara Rug national brochure
Projects listed in *Showcase of Interior Design, Midwest Edition (vol. 1)*
Baker Furniture Catalogue

LEFT: Classic elements of black and white marble and cherry wood tones are enhanced by a subdued color climate.

BELOW: A custom designed farm table expands to seat 14 in this adaptation of a country French kitchen.

OPPOSITE: Dramatic accessories, luxurious fabrics, hi-tech lighting and audio/video balance wit and whimsy with the architectural character of this classic library.

NATURAL WONDERS
BESTIARY
INTERIOR DESIGN
BEST
HG

G/S Design Portfolio

GERMAINE WARNECKE, ISID
43 WEST SLADE STREET
PALATINE, IL 60067
(708)359-1662

SELDA TREIBER, ISID

■ *Our style reflects permanence, contentment and refinement. Each environment encompasses a unique lifestyle, which becomes the hypothesis for our design. We complicate the premise with diversity of pattern, texture and color. Enthusiasm and interaction with the client at the beginning, as well as the end of each project, underscores our true enjoyment of and commitment to interior design.* ■

PROJECTS:
Private Residences: Chicago, Lake Forest, Barrington, Inverness, Oak Brook, Hinsdale, Highland Park and Champaign, Illinois; Texas; Savannah, Georgia; Baltimore, Maryland; Mendham, New Jersey and Wrentham, Massachusetts.

Commercial Work: Restaurants; facility for developmentally disabled children and adults; medical office suites; law offices; corporate headquarters and executive offices.

CREDENTIALS:
Germaine Warnecke:
Purdue University, BS
University of Maryland
University of Indiana
Design Degree: Harper College, Honors

Selda Treiber:
IBM Technological Training Center
Design Degree: Harper College, Honors

Both have served two terms on Board of Directors, Illinois Chapter ISID. They were recipients of Special Recognition for Interior Design Excellence, 1992, awarded by Merchandise Mart and Chicago Design Sources.

Have participated in fourteen Chicago area showhouses, 1983-1992.

LEFT: A European influence contrasted by the use of contemporary acrylic prevails over this eclectic room. Especially noteworthy are the antiques: Trumeau, bronze dore chandelier, large collection of English porcelains and painted leather screen.

ABOVE: A colorful, young look weaves throughout the collection of fine 18th Century furniture and accessories showcased in this sunny surround. The window treatments were designed to highlight the architectural features.

Gayle Shaw Camden

GAYLE SHAW CAMDEN, ASID
GSC DESIGN ASSOCIATES
GROSSE POINTE, MI 48230
(313)885-0767 FAX (313)885-5404

I believe strongly in the integration of architecture, interior design and my client's personal style. I strive for an open dialogue to educate and develop a close working relationship. Creating a timeless, enduring and quality interior is very important to me, with each project being as individual as the client. Good design is as essential as comfort, and I take it as a challenge to create interiors that will satisfy both. An effective designer is an interpreter of a dream, the client's dream —from blueprints to project completion and a nurturer of the soul of both the client and their project. ■

PROJECTS:
Private Residences: Aspen and Snowmass, Colorado; Chautauqua and New York City, New York; Grosse Pointe, Birmingham and Bloomfield Hills, Michigan; Pittsburgh, Pennsylvania; Sarasota, Florida and Great Falls, Virginia .

CREDENTIALS:
ASID, Professional Member since 1975
Art Institute of Pittsburgh, School of Interior Design, 1968
Practitioner of the profession of interior design since 1968

From the same residence, this foyer, living room and dining room show a neutral surrounding in contemporary architecture. Integrated here are antiques, art deco, mid-century and contemporary furnishings, along with ethnic artifacts and an antique savonnerie rug in the dining room.

Pictured here are spaces from the home of a professional couple who live with strong colors in combination with their extensive collection of contemporary painting and sculpture, decorative arts, ethnic artifacts and textiles, Chinese porcelains and antique, mid-century and contemporary furniture.

KEEP TESTING

K. Lasker-Goldberg Designs, Inc.

KAREN LASKER-GOLDBERG
1869 EASTWOOD AVENUE
HIGHLAND PARK, IL 60035
(708) 831-5868 FAX(708) 831-5871

Design is bringing a masterly touch to the ordinary, it is a sensual experience, the feel of fabrics, the explosion or calmness of color, the cold textures of metal, the warmth of wood, the heat of brilliant lighting, the coolness of a controlled environment.

In creating that special, one-of-a-kind interior I bring my professional expertise to the unique relationship of designer-client.

I translate the client's view into a design reality. I utilize space planning, lighting design, custom furniture, coordination of surface materials with consideration towards the human presence.

I listen carefully to the clients, their priorities, budget requirements and tastes..together we create a plan, a goal, a vision. ■

ABOVE: Hand painted fabric on custom seating scaled for a taller client, faux finish table with inlaid copper and a built in bar with a whimsical etched mirror reflecting the client's athletic accomplishments.

LEFT: An eclectic composition using bold strokes of color in the bed throw of royal silk saris and the austere lines of the Biedermeyer antique furniture.

PROJECTS:
Private Residences: Chicago's Gold Coast and North Shore, Illinois; Boca Raton, Florida; Harbor Country, Michigan; Indianapolis, Indiana; Milwaukee, Wisconsin and New York City, New York.

Commercial Work: Medical and dental offices; hospitals; law firms; executive offices; manufacturing facilities; lobbies and public spaces; beauty salons and men's hair salons.

CREDENTIALS:
Master of Fine Arts, School of the Art Institute of Chicago
Additional studies in Interior Architecture and Sculpture
Northwestern University, BA
Guest Lecturer, School of Art Institute - Departments of Sculpture and Interior Architecture
Brandeis University
Illinois Arts Council
Art Institute Affiliates
"Chicago Is", Convention Planners

PUBLISHED IN:
Chicago Sun Times
Chicago Tribune
Chicago Tribune Magazine (four page spread)
North Shore Magazine
Builder/Architect Magazine
Pioneer Press
Suburban Newspapers/Other trade publications

TOP: This interior is governed by a classical style and a restricted palette of colors punctuated by dramatic lines sculpting the space.

LEFT: My inspiration went out the window, captured nature, pulled it indoors and was interpreted into a colorful, contemporary interior of custom furniture, paintings and accessories.

Paul Granata Interiors

PAUL GRANATA
330 WEST DIVERSEY PARKWAY
CHICAGO, IL 60657
(312)883-1930

CHINA

The Green Frog

SUSAN H. BARKER
8970 WILSON MILLS ROAD
CHESTERLAND, OH 44026
(216)729-1111 FAX (216)729-3167

Rooms should be designed to put everyone at ease, comfort being an important connecting link. Antiques lend themselves to this feeling by giving a warm mellow look. I like mixing color, fabric and furniture in such a way that the overall effect is not "decorated."

PROJECTS:
Private Residences: Cleveland, Ohio; New York; Florida; Martha's Vineyard in Massachussets; London and Hong Kong.

Commercial Work: Executive offices, corporate headquarters, country clubs and historic landmarks.

CREDENTIALS:
Centenary College
Robin Hill Ltd., Hudson, Ohio

ANTIQUES

Bruce Gregga Interiors, Inc.

BRUCE GREGGA
1203 NORTH STATE PARKWAY
CHICAGO, IL 60610
(312)787-0017

Interiors have to work for the people who live in them. They should be an extension of a person's self, a reflection of his or her lifestyle, not the designer's "design statement."

PROJECTS:
Private Residences: Chicago, New York and London.

Commercial Work: Whitehall Hotel; Ultimo, a retail specialty clothing store; The Standard Club; Greenacres Country Club; McDonald's Restaurants and the corporate office of a multi-franchise McDonald's Restaurant owner; and the lobby of Watertower Place.

CREDENTIALS:
ASID, Professional Member
Formica Corporation Design Advisory Board
Resources Council Annual Product Design Award Competition, Judge
Cooper Hewitt Museum Decorative Arts Advisory Committee
Smithsonian Institution's National Museum of Design
Residential Design Excellence Award, Chicago Design Sources
Interior Design Hall of Fame
Grand Prix Award, the International Linen Confederation
"Dean of Design," Chicago Design Sources
"*Architectural Digest* at the Smithsonian," Speaker
"*AD 100*"
Who's Who in Interior Design

PUBLICATIONS:
Architectural Digest
Bon Appetit
House Beautiful
HG
Interior Design

BELOW: Mr. Gregga's careful selection of color and materials form an ideal setting for artwork in this Chicago apartment's dining room. Horses are by Deborah Butterfield; Dale Chihuly glass and William Morris vase are on the buffet.

OPPOSITE: A Lucas Samara wire sculpture, along with a pair of Ed Paschke paintings and a blue glass vase by Dan Dailey, are points of focus in the design of the same apartment's living room.

GUNKELMANS

R. THOMAS GUNKELMAN
1112 HARMON PLACE
MINNEAPOLIS, MN 55403
(612)333-0526 FAX (612)333-0528

Gunkelmans, an interior design studio located in Minneapolis, has been creating interior environments for Twin City residents for 24 years.

Satisfied clientele throughout the country attest to Gunkelmans approach to the design of homes, shops and offices.

Each client is the inspiration for Gunkelmans Interior Design. Fulfilling the client's requirements in the most creative way is the end result. ■

RIGHT: Sofa designed by R. Thomas Gunkelman, Roebuck/Farrell residence.

BELOW: Applebaum residence, Minneapolis.

PROJECTS:
Private Residences: Minneapolis, Minnetonka, St. Paul and Detroit Lakes, Minnesota; Naples and Tampa, Florida; New York City; Los Angeles and San Francisco, California; Chicago, Illinois and Mexico City.

Commercial Work: Various professional offices of residential clients.

CREDENTIALS:
ASID, Professional Member
Degree in Business and Design, North Dakota State
Residential, Interior Design Excellence, Chicago, Design Mart, 1986
ASID Designer of Distinction, Minnesota Chapter
26 various awards from competitions sponsored by the Minnesota Chapter of ASID

PUBLISHED IN:
Minneapolis/St. Paul Magazine
Architecture Minnesota
Star Tribune Minneapolis
International Homes
Minnesota Monthly

ABOVE: Residence, New York City.

LEFT: Custom designed bath for private residence.

HARRIS DESIGN ASSOCIATES

NANCY HARRIS-HELTNE
6278 CHASEWOOD DRIVE
MINNEAPOLIS, MN 55344
(612)943-1616 FAX(612)943-0201

We design spaces that complement the architecture and enhance each client's individual style.

It is our design practice to work as a team with the architect, contractor and the client.

Communication, attention to detail, staying within the budget and reliability make our projects a success. ■

PROJECTS:
Private Residences: Minnesota; Wisconsin; Omaha, Nebraska; Florida and Arizona.

Commercial Work: Restaurants, corporate headquarters and health club facilities.

Richard Himmel

RICHARD HIMMEL
1800 MERCHANDISE MART
CHICAGO, ILLINOIS 60654
(312) 527-5700 FAX (312)527-2169

Projects: Commercial Work: Playboy Club and Resort in Lake Geneva, Wisconsin; Marbury Place Hotel in Washington, D.C.; and installations for Victoria's Secret and the Limited clothing store chain. Designed upholstered furniture for Dods-Murdick Transitional Furniture and Baker Furniture Company and Interior Crafts, Incorporated. Country clubs, corporate aircraft, yachts, railroad cars, restaurants, banks and embassies.

CREDENTIALS:
University of Chicago
ASID, Fellow
ASID, former Midwest Chapter President
ASID Designer of Distinction Award, 1992
Interior Design Magazine Hall of Fame
Dean of Dean Design Award, 1987
Euster Award For Outstanding Contributions to the Interior Design Industry, 1982

PUBLISHED IN:
Architectural Digest Interior Design
Interiors
HG
The Chicago Tribune
The Chicago Sun Times
The New York Times
Numerous other interior design publications

MARINO
1959

INEZ SAUNDERS AND ASSOCIATES, INC.

INEZ SAUNDERS
449 NORTH WELLS STREET
CHICAGO, IL 60610
(312)329-9557 FAX (312)329-9093

Our goal is to meet and succeed in reaching the individual needs and tastes of each of our clients. To obtain this goal, we keep in close communication with our clientele and run a very professional and efficient office. ■

PROJECTS:
Private Residences: Chicago, Illinois and surrounding suburbs; California; Florida; Michigan; New York and Washington D.C.

Commercial Work: Restaurants, stores, lobbies and hallways and model apartments.

PUBLISHED IN:
Architectural Digest
House Beautiful
HG
North Shore Magazine
Better Homes and Gardens
The Chicago Tribune
Chicago Sun Times

TOP: A contemporary high-rise provides a dramatic backdrop for elegant living.

BOTTOM: The addition of a sunroom provides a visual connection to the outdoors and gives an open feeling to this home.

ABOVE: Renovated Old World living-dining room now exists in what was once a high school classroom.

Interiors By Design, Inc.

BARBARA M. GIMESKY
134 WEST UNIVERSITY DRIVE, SUITE 317
ROCHESTER, MICHIGAN 48307
(313) 656-2272 FAX: (313) 656-8667

BEVERLY J. HARDER

PROJECTS:
Private Residences: Rochester, Birmingham, Bloomfield Hills, Clarkston, Metamora, Traverse City and Harbor Springs, Michigan; Boca Raton, Florida; Washington, D.C.; McLean, Virginia; Carolina Trace, North Carolina; Scottsdale and Phoenix, Arizona; Laguna Niguel and Newport Beach, California and Chicago, Illinois.

Commercial Work: Allied Automotive; Ford Motor Company; Century 21 Real Estate Offices; Dynamic Associates; Pepsi Cola Company; Rochester Community House; City of Rochester Municipal Offices; University of Detroit Jesuit High School; Vertech Corporation; numerous physicians, dentists and medical offices.

CREDENTIALS:
ASID, Allied Member
IFDA
IDS
University of Maryland, School of Fine Arts
Wayne State University Interior Design
Junior League of Detroit Designer Showhouse, 1988, 1990, 1992, Grosse Pointe, Michigan
Detroit Symphony Orchestra Designer Showhouse, 1989
Rochester Symphony Designer Showhouse, 1991

PUBLICATIONS:
Detroit News Homestyle
Century 21 Preferred Client
Style
The Jewish News
Grosse Pointe News
New Housing of Michigan

■ *Our philosophy, simply stated, is expressed in unique and timeless interiors that are exciting and always executed professionally and in good taste.*

We sincerely believe that the foundation of a successful project is the relationship that evolves between the designer and client as we create an environment that reflects the client's lifestyle with classic refinement.

Our firm has a strong reverence for the past, a love and celebration of the present and a total commitment to excellence in design for the future. ■

RIGHT: Hand-screened wall coverings, imported fabrics and trim, a restored Louis XVI trumeau mirror(circa 1840) and a rare French curio join forces to give this otherwise small sitting room (off the powder room) an importance of its own.

OPPOSITE ABOVE: This cheery sun porch boasts a trompe l óeil sky on the ceiling. The whimsical vine and bittersweet application at the windows leaves the beautiful lake view unobstructed.

OPPOSITE BELOW: Warm colors, hand-painted faux marbré walls and collected furnishings combine to create an electric, yet traditional ambiance for this inviting gathering room.

James R. Irving, ASID

JAMES R. IRVING, ASID
13901 SHAKER BLVD.
CLEVELAND, OH 44120
(216)283-1991 OR (216)751-1100

My great passion is designing beautiful rooms. As a colorist-decorator, it is most important to capture the essence-persona of the client. Color and room arrangement are utmost. And I enjoy doing every last minute detail. My client list includes second and third generations of the same family.

James R. Irving, ASID

PROJECTS:
Private Residences: Cleveland, Ohio; Bermuda; Washington D.C.; New York; Chicago and Richmond, Virgina.

Commercial Work: Designer showhouses, corporate offices, country clubs and churches in the Cleveland area and throughout the U.S. and abroad.

CREDENTIALS:
ASID
Western Reserve University
New York School of Interior Design
Intstitute of Rome

Brian Killian & Co

BRIAN J. KILLIAN
211 NORTH WOODWARD AVENUE
BIRMINGHAM, MI 48009
(313)645-9801 FAX(313)645-8619

. . . GOD SEES YOU, BUT HE UNDERSTANDS

KLINGMANS OF GRAND RAPIDS

AL DICKERSON, ASID, IIE
3525 28TH STREET S.E.
GRAND RAPIDS, MI 49512
(616)942-7300 FAX(616)942-1957

My goal is a comfortable and practical environment for my client's living and working activities. Whether new construction or remodel, my greatest strength is working with the client's architects or builders. An effective designer listens and interprets their client's needs and dreams, helping them to achieve the finished project while avoiding the difficulties associated with building and decorating. Creating a uniquely beautiful space is the frosting on the cake.

PROJECTS:
Private Residences: Michigan; Indiana; Ohio; Wisconsin; Florida; Arizona; California; Hawaii; Colorado; Idaho.

Commercial Work: Banks, legal and medical offices, country clubs, model homes and yacht design.

CREDENTIALS:
Industrial Engineering BSE and Business MBA, The University of Michigan
New York School of Interior Design
Licensed residential builder, State of Michigan
American Society of Interior Designers
Marquis Who's Who, Midwest Edition
Barron's Who's Who in Interior Design, International Edition

PUBLISHED IN:
Woman's Day Magazine
Collectibles Market Guide
Colorado Interiors
Homestead Gazette
The Grand Rapids Press

LEFT: The owner's multitude of collections and love of color are expressed.

BELOW: A porch is now correspondence, game and bar multifunctions.

OPPOSITE: Permanent murals set the color palette, individual dining tables counterbalance formality.

Joan Knight Interiors

JOAN A. KNIGHT
26561 WEST TWELVE MILE ROAD
SOUTHFIELD, MI 48034
(313)354-5365 FAX (313)354-7032

MAGGIE M. FRANKLAND
LANSING OFFICE
(517)337-0863

Our vast diversification in interior design begins with listening, establishing a rapport with each client, evaluating their desires and creating for each one livability, comfort and balance. This harmony is achieved through a close relationship of architecture and interior design. Whether it requires the use of treasured old pieces or searching for the new and unusual, we create a unique blend from an abundance of resources. This exploration and exchange of ideas between client and designer is our key to the warmth and graciousness our clients desire. Extensive experience in restoration and antiques is an additional benefit. ■

RIGHT: Northern Michigan dining room with custom rug and antler chandelier. Furniture created from European estate lumber.

BELOW: Carved "Elephant Bed" from Kenya with Asian art treasures are enhanced by the tunnel lighting of this Harold Turner home. (Harold Turner was a craftsman to Frank Lloyd Wright.)

OPPOSITE: Custom design on hand tufted stair runner. Concealed lighting from stucco sconces.

PROJECTS:
Private Residences: Michigan, Colorado, New York and Chicago, Illinois.

Commercial Work: Supreme Court Lobby, State of Michigan; Public Sector Consultants; McGinty Brown Law Firm; restaurants and various medical and dental offices.

CREDENTIALS:
University of Detroit
Graphic Arts/Fisher Body & Chrysler Corporation
Junior League of Detroit Showhouses, 1988, 1990, 1992
Detroit Symphony Designer Showhouse, 1989, 1993
International Home Fashions Show

PUBLISHED IN:
Style
Detroit News
Grosse Pointe News
Detroit Free Press
New Housing
Eccentric

OPPOSITE: Entire guest quarters reflect the 17th Century Robert Adams fireplace.

ABOVE: Architectural lines closely followed in the custom designs.

LEFT: Contemporary elegance for a Robert Stern master bath design.

Carol R. Knott Interior Design

CAROL R. KNOTT
430 GREEN BAY ROAD
KENILWORTH, IL 60043
(708)256-6676

■ *My responsibility is to interpret the client's wishes and desires. Through open communication, we first identify a concept of how they would like to live. I then strive to implement the design process in a professional manner. I know I have done my part when the client is thrilled with the end result and I feel personally rewarded.* ■

PROJECTS:
Private Residences: Apartments and vacation homes in Chicago's Gold Coast, Lincoln Park area, North Shore, Barrington and Hinsdale, Illinois; Wisconsin; Michigan; Greenwich, Connecticut; Staunton, Virginia; New Jersey; West Virginia; Hilton Head, South Carolina; Fort Lauderdale and Naples, Florida; San Francisco, California; Phoenix, Arizona; Canada; and Portugal.

Commercial Work: Executive offices and medical suites.

CREDENTIALS:
ASID, Professional Member
Registered Interior Designer, State of Illinois
ASID, Illinois Chapter Board of Directors, 2 years
Chicago Designer Club
Northwestern University, 1966
The Academy of Lighting Arts, 1966
Interior Design Advisory Panel, 1978
American Institute of Interior Designers, 1970
Who's Who of American Women
Who's Who in the Midwest
Who's Who in Interior Design
Residential and Interior Design Excellence Award, Chicago Design Sources, The Merchandise Mart, 1989

PUBLICATIONS:
Chicago Tribune
Chicago Sun Times
The Pioneer Press
HG
Woman's World
Pierre Deux's French Country
Better Homes and Gardens Decorating, 1981
House Beautiful

Gary Kowit Interior Design

GARY KOWIT
31691 CEDAR ROAD
CLEVELAND, OH 44124
(216) 449-7518

Successful design is a collaboration of the client's needs, dreams and ideas, with style, comfort and beauty.

PROJECTS:
Private Residences: Los Angeles and Pebble Beach, California; Hawaii; Ireland; Bloomfield Hills, Michigan; Boca Raton and Palm Beach, Florida; Cleveland, Ohio; Nashville, Tennessee and New York City, NY.

CREDENTIALS:
Miami University, Ohio School of Fine Arts
Traphagen School of Design, New York City, NY

PUBLISHED IN:
Plain Dealer
Northern Ohio Life
Cleveland Magazine

ALL PHOTOS: Deep seagreen and white create a cool oasis in Palm Beach, Florida.

CHAGALL
CHAGALL

KREITINGER DESIGN

JACK KREITINGER
1512 NORTH FREMONT
CHICAGO, IL 60622
(312)751-8802 FAX(312)751-2377

A beautiful room is all about balance-the juxtaposition of opposites. We like to emphasize texture and down play color, and we like sparse uncluttered rooms that are intimate and cozy. It is the mix of materials, styles, scale, lighting, etc., that excites us. Our decorating style is as varied as our clients, and our goal is to create a room that is both visually dramatic and physically comfortable. The finished room should reflect the client's taste and personality and not be a rubber stamp decorator's room. ■

PROJECTS:
Private Residences: Chicago and suburbs of Illinois; Naples, Florida; Montserrat and San Fransisco, California.

Commercial Work: Corporate offices, retail stores and a hair salon in Chicago, Illinois.

PUBLISHED IN:
Chicago Tribune
Chicago Sun Times
North Shore
New York Times
Decorating and Remodeling
Playboy

BELOW: Textured fabrics and sensuous furniture shapes create elegant comfort in this monochromatic room.

OPPOSITE ABOVE: Trompe l'oeil stone work provides alternative window treatment in the seating area of this neo-classic pool room.

OPPOSITE BELOW: Traditional seating complements contemporary art.

SUSAN KROEGER, LTD.

SUSAN KROEGER
253 FRANKLIN ROAD
GLENCOE, IL 60022
(708)835-5262 FAX (708)835-5292

■ *Continuity, style and classicism are primary to my design approach. It's important to develop my clients' sense of sophistication, serenity, romance and lifestyle in creating for them a well-balanced and relaxed setting. Elements such as light, texture and color dimensionalize the client's collection of objects and furnishings to further the ambience of the environment. This is always accomplished with professionalism and excellence in both design and service.* ■

PROJECTS:
Private Residences: Chicago and North Shore Illinois area; California; Arizona; Wisconsin; Indiana; Florida; Rhode Island and New York City.

Commercial Work: Corporate offices in Chicago.

CREDENTIALS:
ASID, Allied Member
Maryville College, St. Louis, Missouri, BA
St. Louis University in Missouri, postgraduate studies

PUBLISHED IN:
North Shore Magazine
Chicago Sun Times
The Chicago Tribune
Better Homes and Gardens, special editions

Laura Barnett Henderson, Inc.

LAURA BARNETT, ISID
1632 ORRINGTON
EVANSTON, IL 60201
(708)864-4150 FAX (708)864-4170

■ *I always design with the spirit and lifestyle of the client in mind. Whether for a family or a company, this personal attention results in ambience that is both exciting and nurturing. In a contemporary installation, there's a sense of unexpected warmth; in a traditional design, it's a surprising twist of something with a little "bite". In all cases, the finished work expresses vitality, sensuousness, and natural drama, all with great poise.* ■

ABOVE: Shimmering tones of silver, gunmetal and bronze reflect the rhythms and colors of the view — a spectacular sweep of Lake Michigan.

BELOW: Warmth and expansiveness meet in this contemporary living room enriched with authentic Western art and traditional touches.

PROJECTS:
Private Residences: Throughout Chicago and the surrounding area, Texas, Florida, Wisconsin, Michigan and California.

Commercial Work: Law and medical suites, restaurants, hotels, stores, executive and general offices. Clients include Motorola, Wilson Sporting Goods, Marriott, Prudential Preferred Properties, *The Chicago Tribune* and The Museum of Science and Industry.

CREDENTIALS:
ISID, Professional Member and Vice President
Interior Architecture and Design, Chicago Academy of Fine Arts
Special Recognition Award, Chicago Design Sources
Showhouse/Special Project Designer for charities including United Cerebral Palsy, Park, Ridge Youth Campus, Orchard Village and ORT

PUBLISHED IN:
Better Homes and Gardens
Better Homes and Gardens, Decorating
North Shore Magazine
Chicago Tribune
Chicago Sun Times
Pioneer Press
Paddock Publications
Today's Chicago Woman

ABOVE: Drama on the diagonal makes a restful, yet vivacious white backdrop to offset antique carpets, oil paintings and stained glass windows.

LEFT: Whimsy takes a sophisticated turn in this tiny breakfast room with zebra wicker seating, botanical wallpaper and shell-inspired balloon shades.

Lawson Design

LAWSIE PENNINGTON COLER
744 CREVELINGS LANE
CINCINNATI, OH 45226
(513)321-8844

I believe in listening to the client's voice rather than a "look" or "trademark" style.

I interpret and guide key color, style and appropriateness decisions; starting early the design involvement to avoid any major issues mid-project.

Designers need to be realistic and have good business sense for their client's needs as well as for themselves.

Trends do not necessarily represent good design.

I believe in space with personality, reflecting a collaboration between designer and client. ■

PROJECTS:
Private Residences: New York City; Cincinnati, Ohio; Delray Beach and Palm Beach, Florida.

Commercial Work: Corporate offices, schools and private clubs.

PUBLISHED IN:
HG
Cincinnati Enquirer
Cincinnati Magazine

ABOVE: Warm, liveable kitchen.

BELOW: New construction with character.

OPPOSITE: Intimate library from a Junior League showhouse.

Kay Maida Lemke

KAY MAIDA LEMKE
13 NORTH EAST FIFTH STREET
MINNEAPOLIS, MN 55413
(612)331-7040

A well designed environment, either residential or commercial, begins with a concept, as does a fine painting. It is the designer's responsibility to encourage clients to express their thoughts, feelings, ideas and expectations, and then translate that information into their environment, utilizing colors, forms, shapes, textures and lighting. The relationship between the client and designer is a long term collaboration with clear and constant communication. The good working relationship that is required to create this level of design has also resulted in many long term friendships that make the process so very rewarding. The ultimate satisfaction is when the wants and needs of the client have been met and there is artistic satisfaction on the part of the designer. ■

PROJECTS:
Private Residences: Minneapolis, St. Paul, Minnesota and surrounding area; Santa Fe, New Mexico; Clearwater and St. Petersburg, Florida; Westport, Connecticut and Cape Cod, Massachusetts.

Commercial Work: Stylemark, Inc.; Arrow Pontiac; Suburban Chevrolet; executive offices of Burlington Northern; Metropolitan Corporation; medical and law suites; restaurants and art galleries.

CREDENTIALS:
Minneapolis College of Art and Design
University of Minnesota, MFA
University of Minnesota, School of Architecture

WINNIE LEVIN INTERIORS, LTD.

WINNIE LEVIN
595 ELM PLACE, SUITE 202
HIGHLAND PARK, IL 60035
(708)433-7585 FAX (708)433-9353

I am dedicated to creating comfortable, distinctive and enduring interiors reflective of the client's lifestyle.

It is very important to provide my clients with a balance between interior architecture and carefully selected furnishings, while always giving the utmost importance to detail.

The most successful projects always evolve through a close working relationship with my clients, where I can anticipate their needs and wishes and translate them into the kind of home they dream of. ■

PROJECTS:
Private Residences: The North Shore, Gold Coast and other select Chicago areas; Wisconsin; Palm Beach and Boca Raton, Florida; Toronto; and La Jolla, California.

Commercial Work: Executive offices, Board of Trade, Chicago; corporate residence, Palm Beach, Florida; doctor's offices; law offices; and condominium lobbies.

CREDENTIALS:
House Beautiful Top Ten Best Showhouse Rooms Competition

PUBLISHED IN:
Chicago Tribune
Chicago Sun Times
Pioneer Press
House Beautiful
Better Homes and Gardens, Window and Wall
Better Homes and Gardens, Bed and Bath
The Birdcage Book
Showcase of Interior Design, Midwest Edition (vol. 1)

MARC CHAGALL

Lori Lennon & Associates

LORI LENNON, ASID
680 BENT CREEK RIDGE
DEERFIELD, IL 60015
(708)948-1159 FAX (708)948-1185

With 25 years of residential and commercial experience, I strive for total communication to meet clients' needs and develop lasting design excellence.

PROJECTS:
Private Residences: Chicago and surrounding suburbs of Illinois, California, Hawaii, Florida and Greece.

Commercial Work: River Cruise ship Holland/France, Hamilton Partners and Crystal Tree Country Club.

CREDENTIALS:
ASID, Illinois Chapter President, 1994
Loyola University
St. Xavier College, 28 reappointments as instructor
First place awards from March of Dimes, Showhouses
National Kohler Competition, Art Achievement from Lourdes Alumnae.

PUBLISHED IN:
Chicago Tribune
Chicago Sun Times
Pioneer Press
Better Homes and Gardens
Kitchen & Bath
North Shore
Window Fashions

TOP: Traditional furnishings and antiques fill this room with walnut paneling and windows retrieved from a late 1800's board of directors room. Additional millwork designed to accommodate bookcases, and conceal television and computer area.

RIGHT: Adding beams with colorful painted designs and the braided cornice window treatment, created the intimate casual comfort required for this spacious 12-foot ceiling traditional breakfast room.

OPPOSITE: Criteria; Create intimate dining, and an exciting architectural space to disguise oversize ducts. With the use of bold colors, innovative designing accomplished!

MARGARET MCERLEAN INTERIORS

GATES MILLS, OH 44040

McGowen Associates, Inc.

NANCY MCGOWEN
311 WALNUT BOULEVARD
ROCHESTER, MI 48307
(313) 651-7630 FAX (313) 651-2505

I believe in creating a comfortable, timeless environment which reflects my client's needs and visions. Attention to detail, fine quality and an emphasis on custom work are fundamental. By sharing the creative process of each project with my clients, I am able to develop an integration of their lifestyle and living space. By the end, the project results are as unique as the client. ■

BELOW: Turn of the century farmhouse parlor furnished with three generations of family antiques.

RIGHT: Architectural detailed doorway entering parlor complemented with antique rugs.

PROJECTS:
Private Residences: Rochester, Bloomfield Hills, Birmingham, Metamora and President's Residence - Oakland University of Rochester, Michigan; Naples, Florida; Pemaquid Point, Maine; Cincinnati and Canfield, Ohio.

Commercial Work: Dental offices, ladies apparel stores and 22 Harbor Restaurant, Grand Haven, Michigan.

CREDENTIALS:
ASID, Allied Member
Ohio State University
Youngstown State University
Design Associate Member - National Trust for Historic Preservation
Junior League Showcase House
Homearama Showcase Projects
Meadowbrook Hall Designer Projects

PUBLISHED IN:
Colonial Homes
Detroit Monthly Magazine
Oakland Life Magazine
Oakland Press
The Detroit News

ABOVE: Classic white kitchen and pantry with hand-painted insert tiles, accented with antique cherry table and rug.

LEFT: 18th century fireside dining reproduced in this 1940's New England colonial private residence.

McGowen Associates, Inc.

GUYLENE MARTIGNON
311 WALNUT BOULEVARD
ROCHESTER, MI 48307
(313) 651-7630 FAX (313) 651-2505

Increasingly stressful lifestyles of today have attached new importance to the home environment. As a retreat from a busy world, comfort and order are welcome elements in a well designed living space.

The transforming of space into lifestyle living is defined by timeless design, balance and proportion, fastidious attention to detail and a love of color and fine fabrics. These are the tools of transformation but the key to this process is communication between the designer and client.

McGowen and Associates is totally committed to relationships based on trust, and to projects which reflect the high standards of both our clientele and our firm. ■

PROJECTS:
Private Residences: Rochester, Bloomfield Hills, Troy, Shelby Township, Metamora and Grosse Pointe, Michigan; St. Louis, Missouri; San Antonio, Texas; Pine Hurst, North Carolina.

Commercial Work: Law offices, computer firms and Ideal Office Supply, St. Clair Shores, Michigan.

CREDENTIALS:
ASID, Allied Member
Design Associate Member, National Trust for Historic Preservation
Detroit Junior League, Showcase House
Homearama Showcase Projects
Rochester's Chapman House
Meadowbrook Hall Designer Projects

PUBLISHED IN:
Oakland Press
Detroit Monthly Magazine
Oakland Life Magazine
The Detroit News

All photos private residences

OPPOSITE: 1840 French cherry refectory table and antique Sarouk rug complete this private residence two-story kitchen.

Amalfi

LaBarge, Inc. - Metternich Cole

DALE METTERNICH
1353 BRIDGE STREET NW
GRAND RAPIDS, MI 49504
(616)392-1473 FAX(616)392-5001

■ *Interior design should reflect the personality or philosophy of the individual or organization which will utilize the space. A designer should be a catalyst, making personal dreams a reality.* ■

PROJECTS:
Private Residences: throughout the Midwest and East Coast.

Commercial Work: Orchard Lake Country Club, greater Detroit; Masco Corporation private lodge, Hunters Creek; LaBarge/Marbo showrooms, Dallas, Texas; San Francisco, California; New York, New York; Chicago and High Point, Illinois, restaurants and excutive offices.

CREDENTIALS:
ASID, professional member
Kendall College of Art and Design, Graduate

PUBLISHED IN:
New York Times
Chicago Tribune
Grand Rapids Press
Furniture Today
Grand Rapids Magazine
Metropolitan Home

UPPER RIGHT: "Room With A View". Sun room of summer cottage in Saugatuck, Michigan. Bavarian styled log cabin overlooking the Kalamazoo River, the connecting link between Lake Michigan and inland yacht basin. Mirrored wall reflects the panoramic view with comfortable sofas and eating area for leisure times.

RIGHT and OPPOSITE "Brookby Estate". Unusual L-shaped grand scaled living room designed for comfortable entertaining, quiet areas for afternoon teas, completely adaptable for club meetings and chamber music concerts. Color keyed to accentuate the 1930's gilded paneling and polished parquet floors, both a "must keep".

Meyer Interiors, Inc.

BONNIE L. MEYER, ASID
BLOOMFIELD HILLS, MI
(313)855-1170

The Designer must be able to interpret the individualism, taste and desired lifestyle of each and every client in order to present him with the refinement of his conceptualized self.

Education, creativity, experience, professionalism and sensitivity to the needs of others, enable me to produce a truly custom interior. It is the absolute responsibility of the designer to understand the detailing of architectural elements such as lighting and space planning and to develop a color palette along with furnishings to enrich the days and nights of those who inhabit the designed space.

I embrace color and pattern...they are prolific in my life and the essence of quality design. ■

PROJECTS:
Private Residences: Savannah, Georgia; Chicago, Illinois; Harbor Springs, Birmingham, Bloomfield Hills, Lake St. Clair and throughout metropolitan Detroit, Michigan.

Commercial Work: Corporate headquarters and professional offices.

CREDENTIALS:
Wayne State University, BFA Interior Architecture
American Society of Interior Designers, Professional Member
NCIDQ Certified
Detroit Symphony Show House 1986, 1991
Junior League of Detroit Show House, 1990
Guest Lecturer
Educator

PUBLISHED IN:
The Detroit News
The Oakland Press
The Birmingham Eccentric

Doug Nickless, Inc.

DOUG NICKLESS
118 WEST CHESTNUT STREET
CHICAGO, IL 60610
(312)649-1855 FAX(312)649-1857

Noha & Associates

ANDREW F. NOHA, ISID
1735 WEST FLETCHER
CHICAGO, IL 60657
(312)549-1414 FAX (312)549-1479

Working with the client to produce a home that is both comfortable and conducive to their varied lifestyles is the main approach to my designs. Clean lines, color and interesting scale are the tools.

PROJECTS:
Private Residences: Chicago and metropolitan area, Southern Illinois; Wisconsin; Savannah, Georgia; Hilton Head, South Carolina and San Diego, California.

Commercial Work: Executive offices, country clubs, restaurants and small hotels.

CREDENTIALS:
Andrew F. Noha, ISID:
Drake University, BA
Excellence in Interior Design, Special Recognition Award from Chicago Design Sources and the Merchandise Mart, 1988
Top Ten Designer Showcase House Rooms, *House Beautiful*, 1989

PUBLISHED IN:
HG
House Beautiful
Chicago Tribune
Chicago Sun Times
Better Homes & Gardens, Decorating Magazine
Chicago Magazine
Victorian Sampler
Showcase of Interior Design, Midwest Edition (Vol. I), cover

VERSAILLES
IMPRESSIONISM

Julie O'Brien Design Group

JULIE O'BRIEN
546 SOUTH MERIDIAN, SUITE 300 A
INDIANAPOLIS, IN 46225
(317) 266-0772 FAX (317) 236-9402

"A home is an expression of it's owners; a reflection of their dreams and ideals. Our work, as our clientele, is varied while sharing integration of architecture, use of detail and artistic integrity to create exciting, personal interiors."

PROJECTS:
Private Residences: Indianapolis, Indiana area including Laurelwood, Carmel and Eagle Creek; Chicago, Illinois; Milwaukee, Wisconsin; Aspen, Colorado; Clearwater and Miami, Florida.

Commercial Work: Restaurants, retail and hotels in Indianapolis, Indiana; Chicago, Illinois; Dallas, Texas and Cincinnati, Ohio and medical and corporate offices.

CREDENTIALS:
ASID, Allied Member
Indiana University, 1976
Butler University, 1980
St. Margaret's Guild Decorator's Showhouse, 1992, 1993
Thirteen years in design

PUBLISHED IN:
Interiors
Contract
Interior Design
Indianapolis Monthly
Indianapolis Business Journal - Home Magazine
Indianapolis Star
Indianapolis News

RIGHT: Romantic atmosphere created by hand rubbing iridescent paints.

BELOW: Custom designed rug.

OPPOSITE: Timelessly elegant dining room.

CYNTHIA S. OHANIAN INTERIOR, INC.

CYNTHIA S. OHANIAN, ASID
355 SOUTH WOODWARD #280
BIRMINGHAM, MI 48009
(313)647-7890

There is always more than one successful solution to every project, that is why interaction with the client is imperative. Upon completion, the project stands on its own as a reflection of the client's individual personality and life-style. I cherish the time that myself, as a designer, and my client share in the joy of solving problems and creating beauty like a team; it is teamwork.

PROJECTS:
Private Residences: Michigan; Los Angeles, LaJolla, Laguna and Niguell, California.

PUBLISHED IN:
Detroit News
Detroit Free Press
Style Magazine
Oakland Press
Ile Camera-Grosse Ile

CREDENTIALS:
ASID, Professional Member
BA in Interior Design
Certificate of Achievement in Lighting
Detroit Symphony Show House
Junior League Show House

BELOW: This dining room has beautifully detailed crown molding, painted and guilded. The walls are upholstered with fabric. The room features highly selective pieces of furniture, including the magnificent oriental screen.

ABOVE OPPOSITE: Comfortable and cozy library with fine paneling and accessorized with antique and family mementos.

BELOW OPPOSITE: Elegant living room with precious antique paintings and priceless accessories and lamps.

GREAT ENGLISH FURNITURE
THE TIFFANY GOURMET COOKBOOK

JAPAN A HISTORY IN ART
CHINA A HISTORY IN ART

O'Neill-Harrington Interiors

STEPHANIE HARRINGTON-O'NEILL
TIMOTHY PATRICK O'NEILL
35111 GRAND RIVER AVENUE
FARMINGTON, MI 48335

90 PARK STREET WEST
WINDSOR, ONTARIO N9A7A8
(519) 977-7777 FAX (519) 977-9035

Our clients' tastes reflect an eclectic mix of traditional to contemporary to period styles. We do not promote current trends in their interiors. Beauty fades. Style is eternal. We interpret their desires and dreams into realities, tempered by budgets that are custom made for each as individuals. ■

PROJECTS:
Private Residences: Chicago, Illinois; Bloomfield Hills and Detroit, Michigan; Toronto and Windsor, Ontario; Ocean Isle, North Carolina and Vancouver, British Columbia.

Commercial Work: Micro-Age Computers; Ontario Breast Screening Clinic; Urgent Care Center; Grey and Kilgore Advertising.

CREDENTIALS:
ASID, Allied Members
ARIDO, Provisional Members
Wayne State University, BS
University of Wisconsin
Haystack Mountain School of Crafts
Kendall College of Art and Design

ABOVE TOP: The living room is intimate and regal. The ceiling is clad in squares of silver leaf while the coromandel screen dominates as a commanding presence.

ABOVE: The master bedroom suite walls resemble aged limestone created with plasterwork and hand-rubbed colors by 'Networks' of Chicago.

OPPOSITE: The great room with mellowed oak detailing offers a grand quarry stone fireplace as a backdrop for a 'Bertoia' sculpture.

Doris Oster Interiors

DORIS OSTER
211 EAST CHICAGO AVENUE, SUITE 920
CHICAGO, IL 60611
(312)664-1660 FAX (312)664-9560

"It's exactly what I had hoped for — I just love it!" These words from my client confirm my abilities as a successful designer.

Designers must be knowledgeable in every aspect of their craft, but it is also their obligation to understand the lifestyle and tastes of a client by approaching the project as a partnership.

A compatible professional relationship based on trust must be established since there are long periods of mutual concentrated efforts involved that should be enjoyable as well as rewarding. ■

PROJECTS:
Private Residences: Chicago's Gold Coast, Streeterville, North Shore-Suburban, Michigan and Florida.

Commercial Work: Advertising agencies, residential lobbies, bank executive offices, law firms, medical offices, hospitals, model apartments for Olympia and York Developers, summer resorts and a McDonald's Restaurant.

CREDENTIALS:
ASID, Professional Member
ISID, Professional Member
National Council of Interior Design Qualification
Fully Licensed

PUBLISHED IN:
Chicago Magazine
New York Times Magazine
Chicago Sun Times
Chicago Tribune
Art & Business Magazine

Bobbi Packer Designs

BOBBI PACKER
126 EDGECLIFF DRIVE
HIGHLAND PARK, IL 60035
(708)432-0407 FAX (708)432-0490

I specialize in creating spaces that emanate from the needs and tastes of my clients. Their personal styles are the driving force in the master plan.

My projects often begin with my architectural plan. Then, working in contemporary and transitional forms, I create an interior that is unique to them.

Immersed in architecture and design for the past 14 years, I love to discover resources that inspire new combinations of elements and materials. Fabrics, colors, textures, stones and finishes accentuate the uniqueness of the setting. Combining my discoveries with my customized architectural designs, furnishings and cabinetry, puts my projects in the realm of avante-garde. ■

PROJECTS:
Private Residences: In Illinois: Chicago, Chicago's Gold Coast and surrounding suburbs; Colorado; Arizona; Florida and Cincinnati, Ohio. New construction and renovation.

Commercial Work: Women and men's clothing stores, beauty salons, law offices and medical facilities.

CREDENTIALS:
ISID
University of Illinois
Harrington Institute of Interior Design

PUBLISHED IN:
Chicago Tribune Magazine
Chicago Sun Times Magazine
HOME
Better Homes & Gardens
Kitchen & Bath Concepts
Il Bagno Italian Magazine
L'ambiante Cucina the Kitchen-Italian Magazine

Janie Petkus Interiors

JANIE PETKUS
42 VILLAGE PLACE
HINSDALE, IL 60521
(708)325-3242 FAX (708)325-9351

I believe a good designer-client relationship is based on mutual trust and understanding. By listening to what my clients are saying, I am able to provide an interior that reflects their needs and style. At the same time, it is also my responsibility to use my talents, experience and resources to create timeless design solutions. ■

PROJECTS:
Private Residences: Hinsdale, Oak Brook, North Shore and select areas of Chicago, Illinois; Atlanta, Georgia; Charleston, South Carolina and Washington D.C.

Commercial Work: Professional offices (medical, legal and financial services)

CREDENTIALS:
ISID, Professional Member
ISID Illinois Chapter, President
University of Illinois, BA
Residential Design Excellence Award, Chicago Design Sources, Merchandise Mart, 1992
Design Excellence Winner National Competition - Window Fashions, 1991
ISID National Historic Preservation Award, 1989
Who's Who in Interior Design

PUBLISHED IN:
Traditional Home
Better Homes & Gardens Decorating
Better Homes & Gardens Windows & Walls
HOME
Good Housekeeping
Country Living
Victoria
Chicago Tribune
Chicago Sun Times

Piccadilly Interiors

FRANNIE ATCHISON
13901 SHAKER BOULEVARD #2B
CLEVELAND, OH 44120
(216)295-0664 FAX (216)295-0664

I think of myself as a "creative traditionalist" who insists on quality and form. My goal is to have the project at hand be reflective of the client's lifestyle and personality.

Since good architectural detailing is not always a given, I love combining pattern, texture and "stuff" to achieve an interesting, comfortable and welcoming interior. ■

KASEY WERNER PIERSON, ASID
BEVERLY PIERSON SCHILLING
256 SOUTH ETON
BIRMINGHAM, MI 48009
(313)642-4010 FAX(313)642-2976

Our goal is to give our diverse clientele design that is uniquely theirs. Every client is a veritable surprise and we take delight in understanding and fulfilling their vision. Together we incorporate the concept and its execution to create an aesthetically beautiful environment. ■

PROJECTS:
Private Residences: Grosse Pointe, Bloomfield Hills, Birmingham and Detroit, Michigan; Carmel, California; Utah; Cincinnati, Ohio and Lexington, Kentucky.

Commercial Work: Executive offices, restaurants, hospital clinics and doctors offices.

CREDENTIALS:
Kasey Werner Pierson

ASID, Professional Member
Michigan State University
ASID Showcase House
Detroit Symphony Showcase House
Junior League Showcase House
Rochester Symphony Showcase House

Beverly Pierson Schilling

Professional Women's Network
ASID Showcase House
Detroit Symphony Showcase House
Junior League Showcase House
Rochester Symphony Showcase House

Ray Atkeson WESTERN IMAGES
Jackie Collins American Star
TULIPS PETER ARNOLD

Robert Pope Associates, Inc.

ROBERT M. POPE
400 NORTH WELLS STREET
SUITE 400
CHICAGO, IL 60610
(312)527-2077 FAX (312)527-2079

The opportunity for successful design exists virtually in any space. Our solutions are strong — integrating client lifestyle, personality and priorities. Client needs and desires create a challenging framework for the design process. Through successful collaboration, we create solutions that incorporate function, proportion and scale, color and light. A well designed space evokes a myriad of emotional responses: drama, comfort, formality, warmth and playfulness. We help our clients to express themselves, take creative risks and recognize what will be important to them on a daily basis. ■

PROJECTS:
Private Residences: Chicago, Glencoe, Lake Forest and Winnetka, Illinois; Miami and Palm Beach, Florida; Puerto Vallarta, Mexico; New York City; Bremerhaven, West Germany and Palm Springs, California.

Commercial Work: Baxter Homes, The Habitat Company, The Quarasan Group, Prudential Insurance, JMP-Newcor, Connecticut Bank & Trust, BJF Development, Rubloff Development and Siemens.

CREDENTIALS:
Simpson College
Chicago Academy of Fine Arts
Chicago Design Sources Award
Licensed Interior Designer, State of Illinois

PUBLISHED IN:
Better Homes & Gardens
Chicago Tribune
Pella Window Book
New York Times
Chicago Sun Times
Real Estate News

GAIL PRAUSS INTERIOR DESIGN, INC.

GAIL PRAUSS, ASID
429 NORTH MARION STREET, STUDIO 205
OAK PARK, IL 60302
(708)524-1233 FAX (708)524-1237

Gail Prauss blends her knowledge of fine art, architecture and interior design, to create timeless design for her clients. Her work is influenced by clients' functional and aesthetic preferences with a sensitivity to the interior architecture. Her design ranges from contemporary to traditional, often with the skillful juxtaposition of opposites in form and time. Technical knowledge allows Gail to design custom furniture and lighting in harmony with the space. "Creative lighting design is one of the strongest elements in enhancing the room's mood."

PROJECTS:
Private Residences and Commercial Work: Chicago and throughout Illinois, Michigan and Florida.

CREDENTIALS:
ASID, Professional Member
University of Illinois, BA in Fine Art
Harrington Institute of Interior Design, Associate's Degree
Registered Interior Designer, State of Illinois
NCIDQ Qualified
National Trust for Historic Preservation, Member
Frank Lloyd Wright Home and Studio Foundation, Interpreter
ASID Showcase Homes, 1987 to present

PUBLISHED IN:
Chicago Tribune
Chicago Sun Times
Walls and Windows

ABOVE: The antique mirror becomes a window, reflecting the out of doors.

BELOW: The golden glazed walls beautifully echo the colors found in the original art glass in this arts and crafts dining room.

ABOVE: The architectural frieze,
enhanced with an oxidized copper patina,
is set against faux limestone walls.

J.P. Regas - Bonfee Interiors

JOHN P. REGAS
318 WEST GRAND AVENUE
CHICAGO, IL 60610
(312) 329-0341 FAX (312) 329-0199

Every client has a style and rhythm uniquely their own. My purpose as a designer is to transfer those qualities into their environment, creating harmony between the tangible and intangible.

PROJECTS:
Private Residences: Illinois, Wisconsin, Michigan, Ohio, Arizona, Nevada, California, Florida and New York.

Commercial Work: Illinois, Wisconsin, Tennessee and Florida.

CREDENTIALS:
ASID, Allied Member
Ray-Vogue College of Design
Art Institute of Chicago

LEFT: The reception room of a Gold Coast home welcomes guests with an antique French tapestry and Biedermeier furnishings.

BELOW: White Ash wall panels and floors accented with marble create a unique background for a Michigan Avenue apartment.

OPPOSITE: The dining room of a Landmark Chicago Townhouse calls for appointments as exquisite as its architecture.

Rhonda A. Roman Interiors

RHONDA A. ROMAN-MILLER
2148 SEMINOLE
DETROIT, MI 48214
(313)924-6877

My design philosophy is as diverse as my clientele, with design commissions ranging from residential to commercial and contemporary to traditional.

My goal is taking a client's dream and needs and structuring them into a tastefully designed reality that dictates beauty, comfort and originality.

From the progressive singles environment to the family home, it's important that the ultimate design embraces you, provides serenity and stimulates conversation among guests, as each room reflects the multi-faceted personality and lifestyle of each client. ■

RIGHT AND BELOW: A melody of color, patterns and texture orchestrated with artifacts of various cultures.

PROJECTS:
Private Residences: Detroit, Southfield, Farmington, Ann Arbor, Pleasant Ridge, Franklin, West Bloomfield and Novi, Michigan; Florida; Georgia; Washington, D.C.; California; Kansas and Ghana, West Africa.

Commercial Work: Cobo Convention Center; municipal offices; senior citizen buildings; business and law offices; medical facilities and development models.

CREDENTIALS:
Eastern Michigan University, BA Interior Design
Lawrence Institute of Technology

PUBLISHED IN:
Essence Magazine
Metropolitan Detroit Magazine
Michigan Woman Magazine
Black Enterprise Magazine
Upscale Magazine
Detroit Free Press
The Detroit News
Media Appearances: Channel 2 and Barden Cable

LEFT AND BELOW: Mirrors enlarge the living and dining areas which have an art deco influence alive with color and exotic traditional accents.

Riemenschneider Design Associates, Inc.

ALYCE D. RIEMENSCHNEIDER
122 SOUTH MAIN STREET
ANN ARBOR, MI 48104
(313)930-0882 FAX (313)930-0974

We worked solely on commercial projects until our clients asked us to bring the same design process to the development of their homes. With careful detailing and architectural response, we reflect our clients' personal collections and experiences in the generation of unique, dramatic surroundings. ■

PROJECTS:
Private Residences and Commercial Work: Residences, corporate headquarter buildings, libraries, retail stores and churches throughout Michigan, Florida and Canada.

CREDENTIALS:
ASID, Allied Member
ALA, Member
MLA, Member
University of Michigan, Magna Cum Laude
Teacher
Guest Lecturer

PUBLISHED IN:
American Libraries
Commercial Renovation

Bruce L. Roberts Interiors

BRUCE L. ROBERTS, ASID
1014 EAST RIVER ROAD
ROSSFORD, OH 43460
(419) 666-3682 FAX (419) 666-0349

My desire is to create and design original interior projects and execute each one to express a client's taste and lifestyle. To see 'a painting in design' become a reality is gratifying to both client and designer.

PROJECTS:
Private Residences: Cleveland, Defiance, Lima, Ottawa Hills, Perrysburg and Toledo, Ohio; Phoenix, Scottsdale and Sedona, Arizona; Chicago, Illinois; Castle Park and Harbor Springs, Michigan; Boca Raton, Fort Lauderdale, Jacksonville, Key Biscayne, Marco Island, Orlando, Palm Beach, Sanibel Island and Vero Beach, Florida and Riverside, Ontario.

Commercial Work: Owens, Illinois corporate office; Taylor Cadillac and Buick; Holiday Inn French Quarter; Inverness Club; Shawnee Country Club; Findlay Country Club; Sylvania Country Club and various offices and churches.

CREDENTIALS:
ASID, Corporate Accredited Member
University of Louisville
Toledo Museum of Design
Massachusetts Institute of Technology
Pepke Institute of Design (Aspen, Colorado)

ABOVE TOP: Gracious dining and a magnificent view of the river are enhanced by the softness of the silk damask window treatment and custom designed area rugs, bearing witness to the owner's 18th Century antiques.

ABOVE: This library is a comfortable retreat reflecting the owner's love of animals and books.

OPPOSITE TOP: The living room, designed with multi-layered patterns and graceful window treatments, is full of surprises for the eye.

OPPOSITE: A custom designed area rug by Mr. Roberts, along with his selection of fabrics and attention to detail, complements the owner's art, 18th Century antique and porcelain collections.

In memory of Mrs. Caroline Jobst Reimann

CESAR LUCIAN SCAFF, INC.

CESAR L. SCAFF, ASID
ROBERT M. KRYCH, ASID
KRIS M. KOCHER, ASID

9 NANTUCKET COURT
BEACHWOOD, OH 44122
(216)831-2033

777 BAYSHORE DRIVE
FORT LAUDERDALE, FL 33304
(305)561-5588

SOTHEBY'S
CLEVELAND
PICASSO THE HEROIC YEARS

Janet Schirn Design Group, Inc.

JANET SCHIRN, FASID

541 FIFTH AVENUE
NEW YORK, NY 10175
(212)682-5844

401 NORTH FRANKLIN
CHICAGO, IL 60610
(312)222-0017

821 DELAWARE AVENUE, SW
WASHINGTON, D.C. 20024
(202)554-0017

Creativity... sophistication... comfort... classicism... timelessness... individuality... characterize our work. Architectural orientation, lighting and art are important to it.

Excellent design, whether cutting-edge or traditional, is our goal. As is excellent service, whether individual or corporation. Client needs, objectives and attitudes are reflected in each project, creating highly individual personal expressions. ■

PROJECTS:
Private Residences: United States, Great Britain and France.

Commercial Work: Adler Planetarium, Ann Klein, Brunswick Corporation, Chicago White Sox, Georgetown University, Goodyear, Holly Hunt, M&M Club, Masland, Metropolitan Structures, St. Charles Manufacturing, Tootsie Roll.

CREDENTIALS:
ASID, Fellow, Past National President
AIA, Professional Affiliate
International Federation of Interior Architects/Designers, Executive Board
Pratt Institute, BFA
Columbia University, MFA
University of Illinois, Architecture

AWARDS:
ASID National Honor Award
Midwest Honor Awards
Illinois Designer of the Year Award
Halo Lighting Competition Honor Awards
Chicago Lighting Institute Honor Awards
Who's Who
Who's Who in Interior Design
Eastman-Kodak/PPA Honor Award
Merchandise Mart Distinguished Designer Award
ASID National Residential First Prize Award, 1993.

PUBLICATIONS:
Major consumer shelter and trade publication's world-wide
Textbooks
Janet Bailey, *Chicago Houses*
St. Martin's Press, NY

Valerie Schmieder Design Consultants

VALERIE SCHMIEDER, ASID
49 MONROE CENTER
GRAND RAPIDS, MI 49503
(616)774-2022 FAX (616)774-4028

PROJECTS:
Private Residences: Western Michigan and Chicago, Illinois area.

Commercial Work: Michigan and Northern Illinois. Professional, corporate and medical offices; retail and trade showrooms; institutional and educational facilities.

CREDENTIALS:
ASID, Professional Member
NCIDQ Accredited
Kendall College of Art & Design, BFA

Design Team:
Valerie Schmieder, ASID
Diane Hoffer, ASID

LEFT: Attention to detail is exhibited in the marble and cabinet designs.

BELOW: Cheerful sun room is ideal for intimate or large gatherings.

OPPOSITE: Natural textures and materials provide warmth and comfort in this Lake Michigan home.

Standish Design, Ltd.

DEBBIE CLINE STANDISH, ASID
1600 WEST 16TH STREET
OAK BROOK, IL 60521
(708) 573-1409

We are dedicated to creating comfortable, distinctive and enduring interiors, reflective of our clients' lifestyles and objectives.

CREDENTIALS:
ASID
ASID Outstanding Young Member '84
Oklahoma State University, BA

PUBLISHED IN:
Chicago Tribune, Home section
Chicago Sun Times, Home Life
Designer Specifier
Better Homes and Gardens, Windows and Walls

MONET

Sublette Design Group

NANCY SUBLETTE, ASID
1244 WEST CHICAGO AVENUE
CHICAGO, IL 60622
(312)243-9393 FAX (312)243-9485

■ *We are experts in the design of small spaces and in making that space functional for our clients. Although we work in any style, our signature look is an eclectic interior incorporating rich surfaces and textures.* ■

Credentials:
Professional member of ASID
Member of Institute of Residential Marketing
NAHB
B.S. in Interior Design, S.I.U.

Published in:
Professional Builder
Builder Magazine
Kitchens and Baths
Builder Profile
The Designer
Today's Chicago Woman
Chicago Tribune
Chicago Sun Times
Daily Herald
Skyline

BELOW: A bar and TV were discreetly intergrated into a custom cherry built-in that we provided. The client's entertaining requirements were seating for ten which we accomplished with a custom sofa arrangement.

OPPOSITE: My challenge was to visually expand the confines of a townhome with low ceilings and create a space that lives big for entertaining. Richly detailed millwork and mirror create drama in this dining room.

Terrell Goeke Associates, Inc.

TERRELL GOEKE
565 VINE STREET, SUITE 200
HIGHLAND PARK, IL 60035
(708)432-3500 FAX (708)432-3713

The fusion of interior architecture and furnishings is essential to a successful project. Detailing and design of the architectural elements in conjunction with custom furnishings created for the unique needs of our clientele is our strongest attribute. Involvement with the architect in the early stages of the project allows us the greatest flexibility in our talents, permitting us to create a unique space that is a reflection of our client. ■

RIGHT: High-tech desk combines with a semi-antique rug and cherry backdrop in a study of practical eclecticism. The desk's glass top expands the room while providing an uninterrupted view of the bookcase in beyond.

BELOW: A mixture of fun, formal, rigid and non-structured elements, meticulously detailed with custom cabinetry, granite and touches of the client's interest in the whimsical.

OPPOSITE: A dramatic statement with plenty of movement, built upon the illusion of the polished granite facing being pulled from the tile undercoating.

CREDENTIALS:
University of Northern Iowa, BA
Registered Interior Designer, State of Illinois

PUBLICATIONS:
1001 Decorating Ideas, 2 publications
Qualified Remodeler, 2 covers, 4 publications
North Shore Magazine
Chicago Tribune, 2 publications
KBB Kitchen and Bath Business, cover
Numerous *Better Homes and Gardens* special editions:
Quarterly, cover
Decorating, 2 publications
Kitchen & Bath Remodeling Ideas, cover
Remodeling
Bedroom and Bath Ideas
Plan Home Ideas

ABOVE LEFT: A totally custom room to accommodate the specific needs of the client and space. Details include a concealed switch and control panel, with security remote pop-up TV, surround sound and custom sofa.

BELOW LEFT: A project developed from conception to create a soft, but dramatic space. The fireplace was built to add strength and movement from one space to the other.

ABOVE: A perfect example of collaboration between designer and architect from the conception of a project. Radius steps emulate the piano contour. Architectural elements and the furnishings continue these lines.

LEFT: Custom finishes and furnishings highlight addition and remodeled kitchen created to let the family enjoy view of exterior landscaping.

Roz Travis Interiors

ROZ TRAVIS
1653 MERRIMAN ROAD, SUITE 109
AKRON, OH 44313
(216) 836-1829 FAX (216) 836-7904

CLEVELAND, OH
(216) 831-5534

NAPLES, FL
(813) 263-0606

■ *Good design is timeless. My role, as a designer, is to guide the client in fulfilling the needs of their lifestyles, in creating the best utilization of space.*

I am proud that I'm known for my extraordinary attention to detail and total completeness of design. ■

PROJECTS:
Private Residences: Akron, Canton, Cleveland, Aurora and Hudson, Ohio; New York; Dana Point, California; Naples, Florida and the Grand Cayman Island.

Commercial Work: Banking facilities; country clubs; medical offices; sports complexes and legal offices.

CREDENTIALS:
Graduate of Ohio State University
Post graduate work in Florence, Italy
Finalist in *House Beautiful Magazine*, Best Decorator Showhouse Rooms

PUBLISHED IN:
Professional Home Builder's
Cleveland Plain Dealer
Akron Beacon Journal
Canton Repository
Country Home
Home and Condo
Unique Homes

Virginia Vallière Interior Design

VIRGINIA (GINNY) VALLIÈRE
BOX EIGHT
BIRMINGHAM, MI 48012-0008
(810) 954-0395 FAX (810) 954-0396

■ *Creating aesthetically inviting and liveable surroundings, with an emphasis on the timeless comfort of European country, are the fundamental elements of my work. Through a background in interior architecture, I design spaces that create settings for the play of antiques, collected possessions, hand-painted tiles and the colorful blend of fabric patterns and textures.* ■

PROJECTS:
Private Residences: Birmingham, Bloomfield Hills, Grosse Pointe Farms, East Grand Rapids, Harbor Springs and Mackinac Island, Michigan; Chicago, Illinois; Coconut Grove, Florida and Buckhead, Georgia.

COMMERCIAL WORK:
Lilac Tree Hotel, Mackinac Island, Michigan.
Various private offices for physicians, dentists and attorneys in Oakland and Macomb county, Michigan.

CREDENTIALS:
University of Michigan, School of Art, Interior Architecture and Design, BFA
Center for the Creative Studies

PUBLISHED IN:
Marketplace, cover
Style
Traverse Magazine
The Detroit News
Detroit Free Press

LEFT: French blue moire walls with slate floor evoke a European garden powder room.

ABOVE: Lace canopy draperies enhance the lakefront view of this summer cottage bedroom.

OPPOSITE: Hand-glazed butter yellow walls complement French antique furniture and faience collection.

OPPOSITE: Hand-painted floor tiles and vibrant fabrics create a sunny morning room retreat.

VASSA, INC.
1923 NORTH HALSTED
CHICAGO, IL 60614
(312) 664-5800 FAX (312) 649-8017

■ *Empathic design, or the ability to identify with my client's thoughts and feelings is my primary goal. The results of any design project depend on how closely I can identify with the client's needs, hopes and dreams. Only then can the specifics of taste, style, technology and creativity come into play with real meaning.* ■

PROJECTS:
Private Residences: Chicago's Gold Coast, Lincoln Park, Illinois, Western suburbs and North Shore areas; Boca Raton, Florida; Palm Springs and Bel-Air, California; Atlanta, Georgia and weekend retreats and summer homes throughout the Midwest.

Commercial Work: Law offices, medical and dental offices, corporate and executive offices and retail stores.

CREDENTIALS:
ISID, Founding Member
Registered Interior Designer, State of Illinois
Who's Who in the World
Who's Who in the Midwest
Who's Who of American Women

PUBLISHED IN:
Interior Design
House Beautiful
Chicago Tribune
Chicago Sun Times
North Shore Magazine
Numerous other consumer and trade publications

Vert and Associates

NANCY P. VERT, ASID
814 NORTH FRANKLIN
CHICAGO, IL 60610
(708)655-1193

9900 VINEYARD CREST
BELLEVUE, WA 98004
(206)455-8400

Vert and Associates' projects are the result of the unique integration of architecture, art, finishes, materials and most importantly, our client's personal style. The successful combination of these elements helps to create interiors that are distinctive, elegant, comfortable and inviting. Through close interaction with our clients, we are able to achieve their design goals while keeping within established budgets and guidelines.

For 15 years, Vert and Associates has used resources from around the world to bring together exquisite and timely environments for our diverse clientele. ■

PROJECTS:
Private Residences: Gold Coast, Lincoln Park, North Shore and the Western suburbs of Chicago; Michigan; Ohio; Minnesota; New York City; Seattle; Florida; San Francisco; Colorado; South Carolina; Oregon and Utah.

Commercial Work: Corporate offices, law firms, hotels, restaurants, medical offices and private clubs.

Lewis Wallack and Associates, Inc.

LEWIS M. WALLACK
5150 THREE VILLAGE DRIVE
LYNDHURST, OH 44124
(216)461-1181 FAX (216)461-1824

Susan Winton-Feinberg/Walter Herz Interiors, Inc.

SUSAN WINTON-FEINBERG, ASID
WALTER HERZ INTERIORS, INC.
2350 FRANKLIN ROAD
BLOOMFIELD HILLS, MI 48302
(313)338-2260 FAX (313)338-8893

PROJECTS:
Private Residences: Palm Beach, Boca Raton and Jupiter, Florida; Short Hills, New Jersey; Toledo and Dayton, Ohio; New York, New York; Detroit metropolitan area, Grand Rapids and Kalamazoo Michigan.

Commercial Work: Yves Saint Laurent, Short Hills, New Jersey; Gucci, Troy, Michigan; Krizia, Palm Beach, Florida; Hattie, Inc., Birmingham, Michigan; Knollwood Country Club, Bloomfield Hills, Michigan.

BELOW: This could well be the living space of a world traveler, but every item in this recently built contemporary home is new. Client of 25 years wanted to be comfortable in a new home, yet have it furnished to create the illusion of years of travel with Old World collectibles.

PUBLISHED IN:
Interior Design
Style
Eccentric
Detroit Free Press
The Detroit News
Detroit Monthly
Oakland Observer
Numerous other publications

CREDENTIALS:
ASID
IFDA
National Builders Association
Fashion Group National Association
Best Residential Designer, Chicago Design Festival
Guest of the Italian Trade Commission, Udine, Italy
Guest Speaker at numerous events throughout the United States

LEFT: Living room of a hexagonal house reveals how color and texture are utilized to reflect Michigan's four seasons within the interior. An eclectic style with soft contemporary colors and Oriental accents is the perfect environment for the clients to display their collection of Asian artifacts.

OPPOSITE: Began working with client prior to construction to design a Japanese contemporary dining room of grand size that doesn't feel like a conference room. Room designed to make guests feel at ease with split glass top tables and urns with flowering plants.

OPPOSITE BELOW: Designed to appear like a living room, this bedroom is part of a guest suite fashioned with a warm mix of colors that make guests feel at home. Recovered sofa opens up into a queen size bed.

ANNE WEINBERG DESIGNS, INC.

ANNE WEIL WEINBERG
982 CHESTNUT RUN
GATES MILLS, OH 44040
(216) 423-0443 FAX (216) 423-0443

PROJECTS:
Private Residences: Cleveland and Canton, Ohio; Naples and Boca Grande, Florida; Dallas, Texas; Memphis, Tennessee and Boston, Massachusetts.

Commercial Work: Bank One and Federal Reserve Bank, Cleveland, Ohio and Sun Media Headquarters.

CREDENTIALS:
Vassar College
New York School of Interior Design

PUBLISHED IN:
C Style
Naples Daily News
Cleveland Magazine
New Cleveland Woman

WORLD FURNITURE

Diane Wendell Interior Design

DIANE WENDELL INTERIOR DESIGN
1121 WARREN AVENUE, SUITE 150
DOWNERS GROVE, IL 60515
(708)852-0235

My primary role as an interior designer is to act as a creative interpreter of our clients' personal style. Through open communication we create an enviroment that fulfills and exceeds their needs and dreams.

Drawing on my experience in new construction and remodeling, I create the architectural detailing which sets the foundation for my selection of furniture, furnishings, accessories and art. ■

PROJECTS:
Private Residences: Arizona, California, Colorado, Florida, Illinois, Michigan and Wisconsin.

Commercial Work: Architectural and real estate offices, banks, corporate suites and retail showrooms.

CREDENTIALS:
University of Illinois, B.S. in Interior Design 1976
Silver Key Award, Homebuilders Association of Greater Chicago
Interior Design Advisory Board, Merchandise Mart, Chicago, Illinois
Charity sponsored Christmas Walks - 1986, 1991
"A Gift for Children" 1993 Showcase House, Burr Ridge, Illinois
16 years of practicing Interior Design
State of Illinois registered Interior Designer

PUBLISHED IN:
Chicago Sun Times
Showcase of Interior Design, Midwest Edition (vol. 1)
Local newspapers

ABOVE OPPOSITE: Octagonal, turreted ceiling transforms a breakfast room from the practical to the entertaining. A space designed for warm welcomes, with white-washed oak ceiling and cabinetry in play with porcelain tile and custom leaded glass.

BELOW OPPOSITE: A book matched marble fireplace creates the theme for an orchestration of textures and design. Silk draperies and brushed leather sofa enter into a dialogue with the custom cabinetry and Berber carpeting, accented by imported accessories in bronze, tortoise and horn.

ABOVE: Plaster ceiling mouldings, niches and dentil ornamented crown moulding transform a new home's dining room into a formal setting of elegance. The custom table revels in the play of light with silver leaf finish and Chinese verde marble inlay, complemented by custom colored display cabinet with gold leaf interior and the brilliance of Waterford crystal and antique urns.

John Robert Wiltgen Design, Inc.

JOHN ROBERT WILTGEN, ISID
300 WEST GRAND AVENUE
SUITE 306
CHICAGO, IL 60610
(312)744-1151

The integration of art, architecture and design is what makes our homes timeless.

CAROL WOLK INTERIORS LTD.

CAROL WOLK
340 TUDOR COURT
GLENCOE, IL 60022
(708)835-5500

A home should look natural, never overdone. As I get to know my clients and their lifestyles, this basic design philosophy is transformed into a statement of their own unique approach to living. I blend classical pieces with the unexpected, and use antiques and touches of whimsy to add interest and personality to a room. Above all, I believe in developing a creative partnership with my clients, advising but never dictating, adhering to cost projections, and offering them a home or office that meets, and often exceeds their expectations. ■

PROJECTS:
Private Residences: Chicago and surrounding suburbs; Palm Beach, Florida; Nantucket, Massachusetts; and summer homes in Wisconsin and Michigan.

Commercial Work: Private offices and executive suites, medical offices, etc.

PUBLISHED IN:
Abitare
The Chicago Tribune Sunday Magazine
Traditional Home Magazine
Better Homes and Gardens, Decorating Guide
Chicago Sun Times
Bon Appetit Magazine

OPPOSITE: Antique Biedermaier secretary with Guatemalan 18th Century Santo in foreground.

LEFT: Master bedroom using antique French architectural panel for headboard. Pillows are made of designer dresses from old European fashion houses. Modern night stand incorporates contemporary style with traditional form.

BELOW: Chicago high-rise apartment featuring an 18th Century Verdure tapestry. Hand-woven rug especially designed for living room.

Howard Alan Zaltzman Interior Design, Ltd.

HOWARD A. ZALTZMAN, ISID
1240 SOMERSET AVENUE
DEERFIELD, IL 60015
(708)948-5734

■ *I endeavor to make the entire design process as easy and enjoyable for the client as possible. The finished product is more important, but getting to the end result should be a pleasurable experience for the client, and not a nightmare of unanswered phone calls and broken promises.* ■

PROJECTS:
Private Residences: Winnetka, Glencoe, Wilmette, Highland Park, Northbrook, Deerfield and Chicago, Illinois; Williams Island and Boca Raton, Florida; and Palm Springs, California.

Commercial Work: Law offices in Chicago, dental offices in Skokie, pension planner offices in Northbrook and country club in Homewood Flossmoor.

CREDENTIALS:
ISID
Registered Interior Designer, State of Illinois
IIDC
Wharton School, University of Pennsylvania, BS in Economics
Harrington Institute of Interior Design, Diploma in Interior Design

Index of Interior Designers

Index of Photographers

■

■